# FISH PROCESSING

*Food Cycle Technology Source Books*

# FISH PROCESSING

**Practical**
**ACTION**
**PUBLISHING**

Practical Action Publishing Ltd
27a Albert Street, Rugby, CV21 2SG, Warwickshire, UK
www.practicalactionpublishing.org

First published 1993\ Digitised 2007

ISBN 10: 1 85339 137 9
ISBN 13: 9781853391378
ISBN Library Ebook: 9781780444055
Book DOI: http://dx.doi.org/10.3362/9781780444055

Since 1974, Practical Action Publishing has published and disseminated books
and information in support of international development work throughout
the world. Practical Action Publishing is a trading name of Practical Action
Publishing Ltd (Company Reg. No. 1159018), the wholly owned publishing
company of Practical Action. Practical Action Publishing trades only in support
of its parent charity objectives and any profits are covenanted back to Practical
Action (Charity Reg. No. 247257, Group VAT Registration No. 880 9924 76).

Illustrations by Peter Dobson, UK
Typeset by Inforum, Rowlands Castle, Hants, UK

# Preface

This source book is one of a continuing UNIFEM series which aims to increase aware-ness of the range of technological options and sources of expertise, as well as indicating the complex nature of designing and successfully implementing technology develop-ment and dissemination programmes.

UNIFEM was established in 1976, and is an autonomous body associated since 1984 with the United Nations Development Programme. UNIFEM seeks to free women from under-productive tasks and augment the productivity of their work as a means of accelerating the development process. It does this through funding specific women's projects which yield direct benefits and through actions directed to ensure that all development policies, plans, programmes and projects take account of the needs of women producers.

In recognition of women's special roles in the production, processing, storage, prepara-tion and marketing of food, UNIFEM initiated a Food Cycle Technology project in 1985 with the aim of promoting the widespread diffusion of tested technologies to increase the productivity of women's labour in this sector. While global in perspective, the initial phase of the project was implemented in Africa in view of the concern over food security in many countries of the region.

A careful evaluation of the Africa experience in the final phase of this five-year pro-gramme showed that there was a need for catalytic interventions which would lead to an enabling environment for women to have easier access to technologies. This would be an environment where women producers can obtain information on the available technologies, have the capacity to analyse such information, make technological choices on their own, and acquire credit and training to enable the purchase and operation of the technology of their choice. This UNIFEM source book series aims to facilitate the building of such an environment.

# Acknowledgements

This series of food cycle technology source books has been prepared at the Intermediate Technology Development Group (ITDG) in the United Kingdom within the context of UNIFEM's Women and Food Cycle Technologies specialization.

During the preparation process the project staff contacted numerous project directors, rural development agencies, technology centres, women's organizations, equipment manufacturers and researchers in all parts of the world.

The authors wish to thank the many agencies and individuals who have contributed to the preparation of this source book. Special thanks are owed to the International Labour Organization (ILO), the Food and Agriculture Organization of the United Nations (FAO), the United Nations Children's Fund (UNICEF), the Economic Commission for Africa (ECA), the German Appropriate Technology Exchange (GATE/GTZ), the *Groupe de Recherche et d'Echanges Technologiques* (GRET), the Royal Tropical Institute (KIT), the International Development Research Centre (IDRC), the Natural Resources Institute (NRI), Appropriate Technology International (ATI), the Institute of Development Studies at Sussex University (IDS), and the Save the Children Fund.

The preparation of the source books was funded by UNIFEM with a cost-sharing contribution from the Government of Italy and the Government of the Netherlands. UNIFEM is also grateful to the Government of Italy, via the Italian Association of Women in Development (AIDOS), for sponsoring the translation of this series into French and Portuguese, and the printing of the first editions.

*Ann Maddison*
ITDG

*Keith Machell*
ITDG

*Linda Adams*
UNIFEM

# Contents

# Introduction

This source book will deal with the importance of fish preservation in small-scale fisheries. The term 'fishery' is used to cover the whole of the fishing operation from catching the fish to selling the product. The traditional fish preservation methods described remove the need for sophisticated techniques such as refrigeration, freezing or canning. They include smoking, drying, salting, and fermentation. Boiling and frying, used for short-term preservation, are also covered.

The intention of this source book is to provide consultants who may have no technical or scientific background with a basic knowledge of the principles governing fish processing and the equipment used, together with promoting an awareness of fish curing methods undertaken by women in developing countries. It is also recognized that this book may be useful to fieldworkers who are concerned with upgrading local fish processing practices, but who may not have any specific knowledge of fish technology.

The small-scale fisheries of developing countries play a vital role by supplying most of the fish used for direct human consumption and also by providing a large number of people with a relatively low-cost and nutritious food. Fish is often the cheapest form of animal protein available. In many cases, these fisheries are responsible for between 50 and 70 per cent of a nation's catch. In Senegal, for example, artisanal fisheries provide 60 per cent of national landings. In Peru, the artisanal fleet supplies 80 per cent of the fish used for human consumption (but only about 10 per cent of Peru's total catch (5.5 million tonnes: 1986)).

Small-scale fisheries are characterized by being highly labour-intensive and requiring low capital investment. They are located in coastal areas, or near lakes, estuaries or rivers, catching fish mainly in shallow waters. Improvements to the fishing operation have been introduced, such as the use of motorized boats and winches to haul nets, but there have been few technological improvements to the handling and processing of the catch, with the exception of the introduction of ice and insulation. This may be because, in the past, increased fish production has received far higher priority from development agencies and local governments than the handling, processing and marketing of the existing catch.

There is often a gender division of labour associated with small-scale fishery operations. Women are usually confined to on-shore activities such as processing and marketing where the work will not conflict with other household duties, while the men go fishing. While women are often culturally forbidden from fishing they usually have a central role in the processing and marketing of fish and derive substantial status and income for their households from these activities. The importance of women in small-scale fish processing needs to be recognized, and this document therefore addresses this issue.

Fish is an extremely perishable food commodity. For no other kind of food is there so much observed evidence of serious loss at every stage from harvest to consumption and so little documentation of the overall proportion of losses from fish production (ECA, 1984). Exact assessment of post-harvest loss of fish is very difficult to quantify in developing countries because most of the artisanal catch is unrecorded and is caught by unregistered fishermen. It passes through many hands on its way from harvest to consumption. It has been estimated that 10 per cent by weight of the world fish catch is lost by poor handling, processing, storage and distribution. However, losses in small-scale fish processing are particularly high and can sometimes amount to 40 per cent (ITDG, private communication).

Because fish is a low-acid food which supports the growth of pathogens (microorganisms causing disease) careful handling and rapid processing are essential. The fish is usually neither chilled nor adequately protected from the sun both on board fishing vessels and at the landing site. Basic principles of hygiene may be unknown or seldom applied so that by the time processors buy the fish, it may already have reached various stages of spoilage. Bacterial and enzymatic spoilage is the most important at this stage. Bacteria present on the surface and in the guts of the dead fish multiply rapidly, invading the flesh. By the time there is evidence of slime on the skin and an unpleasant smell, it is too late to take any preventive action. At ambient tropical temperatures, fresh whole fish is rendered inedible within twelve hours (FAO, 1981). Removing the guts and disposing of them properly will help inhibit flesh deterioration.

The longer the processor leaves the fish before processing, in conditions favourable to spoilage, the greater the losses. It is quite common to see 'ripe' fish which was intended for sale in a fresh form being processed as a last resort. Additionally, moist fish is susceptible to damage by blowflies, specifically their larvae, which are voracious feeders. Insanitary conditions on or near beaches or lakesides, where the bulk of the catch is landed are excellent breeding grounds for blowflies. The adult fly will not lay eggs on fish which have been adequately dried, and efficient processing will therefore help prevent this type of spoilage.

Traditional curing is often rudimentary and good hygiene is rarely practised. During the rainy season, when humidity levels are high, sufficient drying cannot be achieved using traditional methods. In such conditions, stored, cured fish will also re-absorb moisture and become susceptible to bacterial, fungal or insect attack.

Products which are sufficiently well-preserved to prevent microbial attack are still susceptible to insect and vermin attack. After the curing process and particularly during storage, beetles are the main insects causing damage to the fish. Under the most adverse conditions, losses due to beetle infestation have been estimated at around 50 per cent (FAO, 1981).

Losses may also result during storage from attack by any animal pests which can gain access. In such cases, attention must be paid to the adequacy of protection for stored fish. Further losses occur during transport and distribution to inland markets, mainly due to the physical deterioration of the fish. This may be brought about directly or indirectly by incorrect handling techniques, inadequate packaging materials offering little protection, and poor processing techniques. An effective approach for increasing the amount of fish available for consumption is to minimize these substantial postharvest losses. Now that fish resources are frequently over-exploited there is increasing emphasis on upgrading postharvest technologies. Overfishing is now feared in the Bay of Bengal, for example, so attention has been placed on funding the development of aquaculture and improved handling and processing (NRI, private communication).

Traditional marketing channels can be complex social systems, not only in distribution patterns (which may involve four or more tiers of sale), but also in the roles played by men and women. Men may not always dominate the management of fishing vessels, nor the women the processing, as sometimes the fishermen may look after the processing of their catch, and the women may own fishing boats and hire fishermen to obtain the catch.

When introducing any improved technology it is important to examine closely the relationships between fishermen, fish processors, traders and consumers since unless women processors have substantial control over the fishery system, any benefits from these technical improvements may flow to other people. In many fishing communities, women take over the function of buying and selling fish and they have accumulated important trading experience. Certain women in Bolivia ('Cholas'), for example, play an almost monopolistic role in fish marketing and derive powerful status from this activity. Not only is it useful to examine the relations between members within the distribution chain in order to assess the likely impact of the technology, but it may be necessary to look at relations among processors and within the household in order to determine who has access to the technology and on what terms.

The location of the fishing ground in relation to the markets may determine the proportions of fresh to processed fish for sale. With no ice or refrigeration facilities available to artisanal fish processors, and in order to sell the fresh fish before it is spoiled, distribution is limited to markets within easy access. For distant markets or those to which access is difficult, the fish is preserved by traditional processing techniques, such as salting, drying and smoking. Taking into consideration poor infrastructure and limited transport facilities, traditional fish processing is often the only option. Unfortunately, in areas where fresh fish is a more desirable commodity, artisanal fish processors, with their less popular cured products, may face fierce competition from larger-scale fish processors who have access to refrigeration and transport facilities.

Here, not only have the limitations of traditional processing methods been pinpointed, but also those outside the control of the processors. It is equally important to realize that traditional processing methods have many advantages. They supply desirable products to local markets and are low-cost operations. In addition, a sophisticated market structure has evolved to cater for these products. To overcome some of the limitations mentioned above, the type of assistance that is needed is unlikely to involve huge financial intervention or the provision of mechanized equipment which may upset the well-established traditional marketing structure. Often small changes, which are within the financial capabilities of the processors, are all that are needed. Such changes may include the provision of clean water, education and training facilities, simple equipment, or basic materials.

Fish processors are not only limited by their traditional methods and by economic pressures, but also by the variable nature of fish supplies. The amount of locally exploitable fish may change due to seasonal fluctuations in fish movements and availability, man-made environmental changes or changes in climatic conditions. In addition, adverse weather, for example the monsoon, may make fishing too difficult. Fishermen may also have other seasonal occupations, such as farming, which interfere with their fishing activity.

The characteristics of fish which affect the way it is processed are its size, oil content and flesh texture (ILO, 1982). If there is a change in the type of fish caught, then the processing technique may change. For example, the introduction to Lake Victoria of East Africa Nile Perch, which are much larger and have a higher oil content than the Tilapia species originally predominant, has brought about the use of a frying technique previously unused in the area (ITDG, private communication).

Improved processing technology has the potential to reduce post-harvest losses, provide employment and retain product acceptability, or make the product more desirable so that fish processors can maintain or increase their incomes and their selling power in the markets. Consumer preference must not be ignored, as it often dictates product quality. For example, in South America salted-dried fish for Easter is preferred rancid (yellow coloration) rather than white.

When the introduction of an improved technology to small-scale fish processing is considered or recommended, not only must the change be requested by the participants and the impact of the technology on their beliefs, values and social organization be taken into consideration, but also the cause of the problem must be identified correctly. Although problems in fish processing may be readily identified, these may not be of critical importance to the processors. The solution might need to be targeted at other areas such as fish handling and hygiene, marketing and transportation.

This source book is divided into six chapters covering general principles of fish processing, and traditional and improved fish-processing technologies. It also illustrates the socio-economic framework surrounding small-scale fish processing activities, with several case studies. A checklist of questions which helps to place fish processing in the wider context of the fishery system (such as food habits, marketing, socio-economics) is included in Chapter 5.

# 1
# General principles of fish processing

THE WHOLE SUBJECT of fish handling before processing is outside the scope of this source book. Its importance cannot, however, be ignored and the following sections are included to provide consultants with a basic background knowledge so that they will be more aware and able to recognize problems. These subjects will be further discussed in Chapter 4. Some pre-processing problems related to the practices of the fishermen are invariably beyond the control of processors, and consultants should contact local fisheries specialists for advice.

Other pre-processing problems related particularly to hygiene and keeping fish cool after it has passed into the hands of the processor can, to some extent, be overcome within a project.

## Spoilage

Fish spoilage is caused by three main factors:

a) activity of micro-organisms (bacteria, moulds and yeasts);
b) chemical deterioration not caused by micro-organisms (breakdown of oils and fats (rancidity), enzymatic activity);
c) attack by insects (blowfly and beetle infestations) and vermin (this term refers to various scavenging animals such as cats, dogs, rats, chickens, crows, fish eagles, or mites.

Each one of these three factors is a complex topic in itself and it is not the purpose of this book to go into too much detail. Suffice to say that there is no one simple solution to the prevention of spoilage. There are, however, basic principles of preservation which can be applied to fish to inhibit and act as preventive measures against spoilage. Centuries-old practices such as the drying and curing of fish are widespread methods of preservation. Before any improvement on traditional methods such as the one above can be suggested, it is important to understand the principles behind the preservation methods.

As soon as a fish dies, it will begin to deteriorate. This natural process is irreversible and the preservation principle is to *slow down* the deterioration, hence increasing the overall quality and storage life of the product. The sooner any preventive measures are taken after the capture of the fish, the greater the chance of reducing post-harvest losses.

To do this it is necessary to control the conditions which influence the activity of micro-organisms, processes of chemical deterioration and incidence of insect and vermin attack.

These conditions include:

1. Good handling practices on board fishing vessels and at landing sites:
   o good hygiene;
   o removal of guts and gills (if culturally acceptable);
   o washing and cleaning with good quality water.
2. Rapid and effective processing:
   o reducing the moisture content of the fish (e.g. drying, salting, smoking);
   o reducing the temperature (use of ice, shade);
   o cooking (e.g. boiling, frying);
   o lowering of pH by creating acidic conditions (e.g. fermentation).

3. Protection from insect infestation.
4. Good packaging, storage and transport practices.

## Effective handling practice

### Raw material quality

Salted, smoked, dried or fermented fish which is of poor quality and unacceptable to the consumer may have been processed by a satisfactory technique. In such cases the quality of the raw material may be at fault. Poor quality raw fish can never produce a good quality final product.

The most important factor affecting the quality of a fish product is the freshness of the raw material immediately before processing. In many parts of the world, buyers often assess fresh fish quality by feeling and smelling the guts and gills and become suspicious of gutted and cleaned fish because they cannot tell how fresh it is. Some consumers prefer to buy whole fish. It is therefore necessary for fish processors to know that the presence of guts and gills accelerates deterioration.

However, if gutting and gilling are carried out incorrectly and potable water is unavailable then it is debatable whether these operations are advantageous. It is thus very important that processors can recognize characteristics signalling deterioration in fish. Some of these are listed in Table 1.

Sometimes consumers look to purchase 'ripe' fish for processing as the flavour is considered desirable and, in some cases, used as a delicacy. Spoiled or low quality fish may also be purchased because it is generally lower priced. Fish purchased in this condition may be subsequently preserved by fermentation, if this is acceptable to local tastes.

Appropriate action taken to preserve the fish during the pre-processing stage, which means right from the time it is caught up to the time it is processed by some method, is the best preventive measure against spoilage.

The main factors involved in spoilage during this stage are as follows.

### Careful handling

The way that fish are caught and handled is important. Fishing methods can affect the quality characteristics of the fish. The use of gill nets, for example, may result in some of the catch being landed with spoilage already under way, as the fish may have been in the net for a considerable period. Similarly, bruising and rough

## Table 1. Freshness characteristics

|  | *Fresh* | *Spoiled* |
| --- | --- | --- |
| Overall appearance | Shiny, metallic wet sheen | Dull, dry, wrinkled |
| Skin tone | Elastic, firm | Inelastic, slack, bloated |
| Smell | Fresh, seaweedy odour | Sour, 'off' odours |
| Eyes | Clear; projecting | Opaque, sunk in head |
| Gills | Bright red/pink colour, fresh smell | Dull, brownish in colour, 'off' odours |
| Mucus coating on the skin | Free-flowing fine lubricant | Coagulated (slimy) |

handling results in tissue damage around which deterioration starts.

Cuts in the flesh will provide an entry point for micro-organisms and insects which will increase the rate of spoilage.

## Good hygiene

Immediately the fish are caught, hygiene is of paramount importance. Certainly *cleaned* dead fish stored in a clean place to prevent recontamination will keep in a better condition before processing than those that have not been cleaned. As soon as the fish dies, internal chemical and bacterial changes occur which begin to cause spoilage. The best way to keep fish as fresh as possible before processing is to keep them alive.

## Temperature control

Spoilage of fish is directly related to temperature. The higher the temperature, the faster the rate of spoilage, becoming most rapid between 30°C and 40°C. Therefore any reduction of temperature before processing will increase the quality of the fish and any product processed from the fish.

## Reducing time intervals

Ultimately, the quicker the fish is processed the better quality the end product will be. This is helped by carrying out fish processing near the landing area.

# Effective processing to inhibit spoilage

## Drying

Although at first sight drying seems a simple process, in fact the manner in which products dry is complex, depending upon the drying conditions and the physical and chemical nature of the commodity. A basic understanding of the principles of drying will prove useful when looking at possible improvements to a system.

Drying requires the transfer of moisture from the product to the air around it. Clearly both the quantity (air flow) and dryness (relative humidity) of the air will affect the way a product dries as well as the nature of the product itself. The relative humidity (RH) of air decreases rapidly with increasing temperature and the water-absorbing capacity of dry air of low RH is much greater than moist air of high RH. It can be seen from Table 2, which shows the effect of heating air on its RH and capacity to absorb moisture, that raising the temperature of air by only 10°C increases its water-absorbing power by a factor of five.

It is important to realize that there are two stages in the drying process: the first removing surface moisture; the second removing internal moisture from the fish.

The rate of drying during the *first stage* is dependent solely on the ability of the

**Table 2. Air temperature, humidity and water absorption capacity**

| Temperature (°C) | Relative humidity (%) | Water that can be taken up by each kilo of dry air (kg) |
|---|---|---|
| 20 | 80 | 0.003 |
| 25 | 58 | 0.008 |
| 30 | 25 | 0.016 |

air passing over the fish to absorb and remove moisture. Air-flow rate is more important than temperature, but in areas of high relative humidity the air may need heating to lower its RH to a level that allows it to absorb significant amounts of water. In general, air with an RH of 75 per cent or more is not able to effect much drying except in the earliest stages when the fish is very wet.

Once the surface water is removed a *second stage* of drying begins in which water is removed from the interior of the fish. The drying rate in this second stage is dependent on the rate at which moisture can migrate through the tissue to the surface where it evaporates. The migration is a slow process so drying rates are lower than in the first stage of drying. The rate of air flow is less important.

The rate of drying in this second stage depends on such factors as:

o the oil content, as oily flesh acts as a barrier to water movement and slows down drying rates;
o the thickness of the fish, as the further the water has to travel to reach the surface, the slower the drying rate;
o the moisture content — the rate of movement to the surface falling as the moisture content of the fish is lowered;
o the temperature during drying.

During the second stage of drying, depending upon ambient air humidities, some heating of the drying air may be essential to reduce the final moisture content to a sufficiently low level to prevent microbiological spoilage. This generally means 25 per cent or less, depending upon the oiliness of the fish and whether salt has been used. As a general guide, if no salt is used, lean fish should lose approximately 75 per cent of their weight during drying and oily fish 65 per cent (FAO/DANIDA III). Therefore, simple weighing of the fish before, during and

after drying is a good method to check for adequate drying. For weighing purposes there are very simple and inexpensive spring balances often available locally.

The size of surface area exposed is also very important, so splitting or opening the fish will increase drying rates. The fish must also be turned periodically.

One other vitally important aspect of fish drying must be mentioned. If the fish are dried at too high a temperature or when the initial relative humidity of the drying air is too low during the early stages of drying, the outer layers become 'cooked' or altered so as to be almost impervious to water. This effect is known as 'case hardening'. Externally the fish may appear dried, but water becomes trapped inside leading to insufficient drying and hence spoilage. The onset of case hardening makes it very difficult to obtain a good dry, final product. Drying temperatures during the early stages of the process should as a general rule not exceed 40°C.

Taking into account local environmental conditions, the factors mentioned above (air flow, temperature, fish thickness) can be manipulated to give a final product that has:

o been evenly dried and is not moist inside;
o a moisture level below 25 per cent;
o a good shelf-life;
o good visual and acceptable eating qualities.

## Salting

The most important effect of salt is the removal of water from the fish flesh to the point where microbial and enzymatic activities are retarded (Duere and Dryer, 1952). Some spoilage bacteria cannot live in salty conditions and a concentration of 6–10 per cent salt in the fish tissue will prevent their activity. There is, however, a group of micro-organisms known as halophilic bacteria which are salt-loving and will spoil salted fish only. Further removal of water by drying will inhibit these bacteria.

The removal of water, which takes place during the salting of fish, occurs because the salt solution outside the fish is of a higher concentration than the residual water in the fish flesh. As water is removed from the fish flesh, salt will penetrate it. If the salt concentration outside the fish is equal to that inside the fish flesh, no movement of water or salt will occur. Once this happens, more salt must be added to the solution so that salting can continue.

The rate of water movement out and salt movement in depends on:

o the concentration of the salt solution;
o the fat content of the fish;
o the thickness of the fish;
o temperature;
o the duration of salting.

It must be borne in mind that the type of salting operation used will depend on:

o consumer preferences;
o availability of salt and cost;
o fish type, i.e. lean or oily.

Salt is variable in its properties, as it is produced in several ways. The main types are sea salt from the sea or lake waters, brine evaporated salts from underground sources and rock salts. These salts will differ in their chemical composition, their microbiological purity and their physical properties, each of which may affect the salted fish quality.

Apart from contamination such as dust, sand, mud and moisture, salt intended for use on fish should have a low magnesium content and few calcium salts, to avoid the bitter taste and toughness imparted by these salts — although the whiter colour obtained may be a consumer preference. Salt itself can carry halophilic bacteria (mentioned above) and these can contaminate fish treated with that salt. Heavily contaminated salt can sometimes be recognized by its pink colour.

Salt comes in crystals or particles of various size depending on whether and how it has been ground. Coarse grain salt (large particle size) will not penetrate fish flesh as quickly as fine grain (small particle size), nor will it dissolve in water as rapidly. Although fine grain salt will be suitable for making brines, coarser grain is more suitable for dry salting, as a condition known as 'salt burn' may occur if fine grain salt is used. This means that the surface of the fish becomes hardened due to too rapid a removal of water from the fish surface, in a similar way to case hardening. The hard surface then prevents both salt penetration and water removal.

The effectiveness of the salting operation for preservation depends on:

o uniformity of salt concentration in the fish flesh;
o concentration of salt solution and the time taken for salting;
o whether or not salting is combined with other preservation methods, such as drying.

## Smoking

The preservative effect of the smoking process results from drying, and the deposition in the flesh of natural wood-smoke chemicals. During smoking, the smoke from the burning wood contains a number of compounds which inhibit bacterial growth, while the heat from the fire causes drying and, when the temperature is high enough, the flesh will be cooked, preventing both bacterial growth and enzyme activity.

Fish may be smoked in a variety of ways, but the longer it is smoked the longer it will keep. The smoked product owes its storage life primarily to the drying and cooking processes, rather than the preservative value of the wood-smoke chemicals.

Two smoking categories can be identified:

o cold smoking, where the temperature is never high enough to cook the fish (i.e. less than 35°C);
o hot smoking where the flesh is cooked (above 35°C).

Hot smoking is the traditional method more widely practised in developing countries and requires a lesser degree of control over the process than cold smoking. The shelf-life of the hot-smoked product is generally longer than that of the cold-smoked product, because the fish is smoked until dry. Generally, the hot-smoking process consumes more fuel than cold smoking. Hot smoking, however, especially where the fish are tented (i.e. hung on spits), greatly reduces the oil content of the final product. Modern smoking techniques do not preserve the fish, but simply produce a smoky flavour.

Care should be taken in the selection of the wood used for fish smoking, as some types of wood, such as resinous types like pine, may impart an unpleasant flavour and taste to the final product. Other types, such as *Euphorbia*, may be poisonous.

In addition to wood, other available materials, e.g. cow dung, coconut husks and sugar cane trash can also be used for fish smoking.

Care should be taken regarding where smoking takes place, as smoking may bring about defoliation (the loss of leaves from trees), where smokers are placed in wooded areas.

## Combined curing methods

Drying, salting and smoking can be used in various combinations to produce a variety of fish products with the long storage life necessary for transport and distribution. Such combined methods are all designed to reduce water content.

### *Examples*

Drying – smoking – drying
Brining – smoking – drying
Salting – drying
Salting – drying – smoking

Specific examples of combined methods of preservation can be found in Chapter 3.

## Fermentation

In hot, humid climates, spoilage cannot always be arrested by dehydration, as it is difficult to keep the product dry. Fermentation is a method which inhibits spoilage within the fish by increasing the level of acidity. During fermentation, the use of salt inhibits the action of the spoilage bacteria and allows the fish enzymes, or beneficial acid-producing bacteria, to break down the flesh. Fermentation can be defined as the controlled action of desirable micro-organisms on food to alter the flavour or texture and to extend the shelf-life.

The use of fermentation as a low-cost method of fish preservation is more commonly practised in South-east Asia and West Africa.

There are many different types of fermented products and their nature depends largely on the extent of fermentation which has been allowed to take place. (Refer to Chapter 3 for examples.)

## Boiling and frying

The preparation of boiled fish products is significant in South-east and East Asia. These products achieve short-term preservation varying from one or two days to several months.

The action of boiling cooks the fish by changing the structures of proteins.

Enzymes, which can cause deterioration, are also proteins and therefore become de-activated during boiling. The process also kills many of the bacteria in the fish. Tra-ditionally, salt is usually added during boiling, and the amount added along with the duration of boiling determines the shelf-life of the product. Fish which have been boiled for a short time with little salt should be treated the same way as fresh fish. It is only when the fish are cooked for a long time with plenty of salt that they will be preserved to some extent. The ad-vantage of boiling is that it is a very simple process which can deter fish spoilage in the short term when conditions are unsuitable for drying. The process also helps to reduce the fat content of the product, thereby decreasing problems of rancidity.

Frying also cooks the fish and dehy-drates the flesh. Fatty fish can be fried in their own oil.

Both boiled and fried products benefit from effective packaging to prevent recon-tamination and insect attack.

## Freezing and canning

Both freezing and canning are relatively expensive operations and are therefore unsuitable for the majority of small-scale fisheries. If either of these operations is to be taken up, it is essential that careful consideration be given to the economics of production, the adequate supply of necessary materials and the appropriate infrastructure, the potential market, quality control (particularly health as-pects) and likely consumer acceptance for finished products.

---

# Insect infestation

---

Before beginning it is necessary to des-cribe how the term 'insect' will be used within this book. There are many types of insects which affect fish quality, and ref-erence will be made only to those of most significance. These fall into two main groups: blowflies and beetles. Within these two groups there are many species and for identification purpose an en-tomologist should be consulted.

The main conditions which determine the extent of insect infestation are five-fold:

o hygiene
o temperature
o moisture content and relative humidity
o salt content
o degree of protection.

Both blowflies and beetles will typically select specific ranges of these conditions for their individual survival (FAO, 1981). In general, tropical conditions with higher temperatures and relative humidi-ties than those in a temperate climate are more favourable to insect development. Blowfly infestation occurs early in the post-harvest chain, when the fish is moist. As quickly as one day after the female fly has laid her eggs, they may hatch into larvae which may then com-plete their development within three to four days. During rainy weather when drying is slow or impossible, losses due to blowfly infestation may be considerable. In general, the more quickly the fish is dried, the lower the likelihood of infestation.

The adult fly will not be able to lay eggs on fish which is adequately protected, for example by netting.

Salting is known to deter blowflies and beetles, but adequate dry salting to pro-tect the fish (9–10 per cent salt concentra-tion of processed fish weight) may give an unacceptable taste, especially if salted fish is not locally preferred.

Beetles will select fish with a lower moisture content than blowflies. These insects are typically inhibited by moistures greater than 45 per cent (FAO, 1981), and will thrive on a typical sun-dried product. The longer dried fish are stored, the greater the losses from beetle infestation. These insects will feed and reproduce on dried fish, finally reducing it to a powder of waste products.

*Fish basket*

## Packaging, transport and storage

Small-scale fish processing may often occur in localities without good transport and road conditions. Whether the fish is transported short distances on foot or bicycle or longer distances by vehicle, packaging is important so that the fish products can withstand the rigours of transport without breaking up.

The different types of container traditionally used for packing fresh or processed fish include baskets, boxes, casks, barrels, sacks and cartons, made of bamboo, coconut matting, wood, jute, metal, paper and plastics. Large leaves, like those of the banana or plantain plants, may be used to line the container.

### Traditional packing

Apart from the suitability of the container to help prevent physical damage, an important consideration is the way the fish are arranged for packing. Traditionally the fish may be stacked very carefully using a particular arrangement to facilitate its transport and distribution.

It is essential that the fish is processed carefully enough to create a product which can be transported. Damage may be brought about by incorrect drying and smoking techniques or by insect infestation. The better the quality of the fish product before packing, the less breakage and loss will occur during transport.

Providing sufficient ventilation is also important. Any increase in humidity levels immediately surrounding the fish will cause them to absorb moisture, encouraging the growth of moulds and bacteria. Occasional re-drying and re-packing will help prevent such mould attack.

Traditionally, fish products are stored in buildings fabricated from locally available materials such as mud and thatch. When no more fish is available for processing, the smokehouse may be used for processed fish storage. In Ghana, unused traditional cylindrical smoking ovens are being used for cured fish storage.

### Traditional long-term storage of smoked fish

Attention must be paid to stored products because of the problems of beetle infestation and the reabsorption of moisture in humid atmospheres already described. Essential quality control measures include periodic checking of product quality, removal of spoiled fish and re-drying every three to four months in the dry season and every few weeks in the wet season to discourage mould and insect attack. The storage area should be kept clean and dry and preventive measures should be taken to keep predators out.

Often smoked fish is stored in a loft area above the smokehouse where the smoke produced during continued processing will drive off insects and keep the products dry enough to prevent beetle infestation. The drying effect of the smoking process is more effective against insect infestation than the smoke itself.

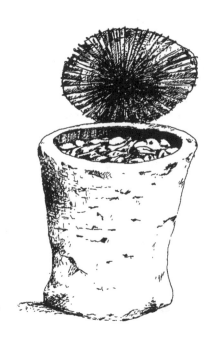

*Traditional
fish store*

# 2
# Traditional fish processing methods

TRADITIONAL FISH PRESERVATION methods have been carried out here for centuries, and even though they have been categorized into drying, salting, smoking, boiling and fermentation, it does not necessarily follow that every method fits into one of these groups. In many countries, the methods used are a combination of techniques. In addition, two processes with the same name may involve quite different techniques when applied in different countries. For example 'smoking' may mean simply throwing the whole fish on to a pit fire in one locality, whereas in another it may involve salting and drying before smoking.

Indigenous processing techniques evolved because of local environmental conditions, availability of raw materials (fish, fuel, salt, building materials), preferences for taste, texture, colour and smell, social behaviour, and economics of production. Each community will most certainly have improved their technique in the first instance by trial and error and perfected a particular process by long experience (FAO, 1970).

This has led to processing methods which have been termed sun-drying, hot smoking, smoke-drying, combined smoke- and sun-drying; salting, salting combined with sun- or smoke-drying or smoking; fermentation and boiling combined with smoke- or sun-drying.

In general, smoking tends to be more common in Africa whilst fermenting and boiling are practised more in South-east Asia. In Latin America the market for and consumption of cured fish products are fairly limited as, historically, fresh fish has been available to coastal populations and other animal protein sources (e.g. red meat) to inland populations. However, there tend to be localized areas of cured fish consumption such as southern Ecuador, northern Peru, and the valleys of the eastern Cordillera of the Andes in Bolivia. Here fish is salted or dried, and consumed mainly during Lent and Easter. Very little control is exercised over such traditional methods and therefore the quality of the products varies considerably.

The following section is intended as a brief guide to traditional processing methods, and is essential background for people introducing improved fish processing techniques in order that the merits and limitations of traditional processing can be understood.

It must be remembered that processing fish using traditional or improved techniques will *not improve* its quality and only serves to help *slow down* the natural spoilage process.

## Drying

Traditionally, whole small fish or split large fish are simply spread in the sun, often laid directly on the ground, or on mats, nets, roofs and sometimes on raised racks. The fish are periodically turned to expose the whole surface for drying. Sun-drying like this does not allow control over drying times, exposes the fish to attack by insect and animal pests, and allows contamination by sand, dirt and so on.

In Malaysia and Java, local fish processors spread their fish on top of mats laid on drying racks and when rain threatens, they roll up the fish in the mats which can then be moved easily.

Being totally dependent on weather conditions, the processors need dry weather and low humidities which are not available in the rainy season. The Food and Agricultural Organization (FAO), reported in 1981 that a typical sun-dried product has, in general, a drying time of three to ten days.

Consumer preference also plays a part in processing methods. Dried fish with a moisture content too high to inhibit spoilage may reflect a preference for moist fish or it may reflect an economic pressure on the fish curer not to over-dry the fish so as to sell a greater weight of water if it is sold by weight, and not by piece or volume (FAO, 1981).

Processors may also sprinkle individual fish with salt and sun-dry. In this case, during drying the fish may ferment slightly to impart a desired flavour, but the principal preservation method is drying.

## Salting

Salting is a traditional processing method used throughout the world for centuries, and it has taken two forms:

o dry salting
o wet salting.

### Dry salting

Dry salting is also referred to as 'kench' salting. In this process the fish are mixed with dry crystalline salt, usually by rubbing it into or sprinkling it on the fish surface, then stacking the fish, making the middle higher than the sides. The water is removed from the fish by the action of the salt and osmosis, the liquid draining away as brine (see page 51).

Another method is to rub or add salt on to the fish and lay them out individually in the sun to dry.

Non-fatty fish are usually dry salted. Large species are split open or filleted. Salting fatty fish in this way will cause extensive breakdown of oils, giving characteristic rancid flavours and smells, and thus is not recommended.

Kench salting has the advantage that water drains away from the stack of fish, so leaving it fairly dry. However, one disadvantage of dry salting is that it may be uneven and that the concentration of salt may be too weak to inhibit mould, bacterial and insect attack.

The fish may not be left long enough for complete salt penetration, and if the pile is not re-stacked to allow rearrangement of the fish, those at the bottom will have been salted to a different degree from those at the top.

### Wet salting, or salt pickling

Pickling is the term commonly used for wet salting and must not be confused with the use of vinegar. The method used largely depends on whether the product will be further processed by drying or smoking, or preserved by salting alone.

Pickle curing starts in the same way as dry salting, in that the prepared fish are layered alternately with dry salt crystals. The fluids are not left to drain away as in kench salting but are allowed to accumulate to cover all the fish. Often, weights will be placed on the top to keep the fish immersed in the brine, and assist in the removal of water (see page 51).

This process is ideal for oily fish, such as herrings, sardines, anchovies and mackerel, especially if the fluids cover the fish quickly, helping to inhibit rancidity by excluding air. A more uniform salt concentration can be obtained by this method giving much less variation in the quality of the product.

The product is often sold in the containers in which it is pickled.

## Smoking

Traditional smoking techniques vary widely. At its simplest level, fish may be placed in a pit containing smouldering grasses or wood, so cooking and flavouring the fish, which is usually charred and has a short storage life. Alternatively, the fish may be laid on racks contained in an oil drum or mud oven, or hung on bamboo sticks in the smoke of the fire.

The pit kiln widely used in East Africa and some of the small mud circular and rectangular ovens offer little ventilation for drying as the fish is predominantly cooked by the heat and flavoured by the smoke of the fire. On the other hand, the 'banda' smoking platforms used in West Africa among other places, may consist of racks raised on poles as in Sierra Leone, or racks placed on top of a rectangular mud platform or flattened oil drum base with openings for the fire (see page 53). In Peru and Bolivia smoking or 'grilling' of split ‾fish is carried out on a wooden framework supported on rocks over an open, smouldering fire. All these systems offer good ventilation, so drying can take place as well as smoking.

The fish, if small, are usually left whole, while larger fish are cut open or cut into steaks and then smoked. They may be placed on their side or, in order to increase the holding capacity and flow of smoke, stacked vertically on their heads. Whether or not the fish have been salted or dried before smoking depends on local availability of salt, taste preferences, and the desired storage life of the product. The longer the fish is smoked, the drier it becomes and the more suitable it is for long-term storage (several months). The examples of traditional processing methods outlined below give some idea of the various traditional techniques used in smoking fish.

The most important advantage of simple traditional ovens like these is their low capital cost. Many disadvantages have been reported, however (Clucas, 1982).

o Constant attention is required to control the fire and turn the fish. This may involve working through the night.
o The operation is both a health and fire hazard.
o Many ovens are inefficient in their use of fuel and ventilation systems.
o There is little or no control over the temperature of the fire and the density of the smoke produced.
o The construction materials used limit the durability of the ovens.
o The open construction of the ovens leaves the fish susceptible to climatic conditions and animal attack.
o The fish product is of poor quality due to insufficient cooking of flesh inside and burning and charring on the outside.

Probably one of the most important limitations of traditional ovens is the lack of an efficient air-flow system which results in poor economy of fuelwood, and lack of control over temperature and smoke density.

## Fermentation

Numerous products are fermented in the presence of salt to prevent putrefaction, and are not dried after salting.

In general, three types of product can be distinguished: those in which the fish substantially retain their original texture, those which resemble a paste, and those in which the fish have been reduced to a liquid. Many traditional fermented products are of excellent quality and their preparation is very skilful.

In South-east Asia, the term 'fermented fish' covers two broad categories of product:

o fish/salt formulations which include fish sauces and pastes such as 'patis' and 'bagoong' produced in the Philippines;

o lactic fermented seafoods produced from fish/salt/carbohydrate mixtures, such as 'burong isda' and 'balao-balao' made in the Philippines.

# Outlines of traditional processing methods

It would be impossible to describe all the traditional fish-processing techniques, but some examples, classified by region or country, are outlined below. These serve to illustrate how local methods have been applied to particular fish types, and the diversity in the combination of techniques used.

| | |
|---|---|
| Region | Africa |
| Countries | Widespread |
| Product | Smoked/dried fish |
| Raw material | Fish |
| Prepared | Small fish are left whole, while larger fish are scaled, gutted and cut up, often without washing. |
| Smoked | Fish placed directly on a trench open fire of dry grass, fibres or sawdust. |
| Sun-dried | Placed in the sun until the product is hard. |
| Product | Often charred on the outside with the inner flesh only partially cooked. Short storage life. Products become putrid quickly. |

| | |
|---|---|
| Region | West Africa |
| Country | Ghana |
| Product | Smoked/dried fish |
| Raw material | Sardines, anchovies (usually small and medium-size fish are used). |
| Prepared | Washed, but not scaled or gutted. |
| Dried | Laid in the sun for five to thirty minutes. |
| Cooked | Placed on grills over charcoal fire inside a shallow circular container. |
| Smoked | Placed in a smoking oven fuelled by firewood and re-arranged periodically for an even cure. Smoking continued until the fish is cooked and dry. Coconut husk and crushed sugar cane are added to the fire towards the end of the smoking process to impart a desirable flavour and colour to the fish. |
| Storage | Long storage life. |

*Source:* FAO, 1970

| Region | West Africa |
|---|---|
| Country | Ghana |
| Product | Fermented fish |
| Local name | Momone/Bomone |
| Raw material | Various species of fish are used e.g. mackerel, grouper, barracuda, sea bream, threadfin. |
| Prepared | Methods of processing differ from site to site but generally they involve scaling, gutting and washing in either fresh or sea water. |
| Salted and packaged | Salting with either coarse salt or brine and dried. During salting, the fish is rubbed with salt and packed in layers of solid salt in various types of containers, including wooden or concrete troughs. In certain areas salt is placed inside the abdominal cavity and behind the gills of individual fish before packing. After packing, the containers of fish are covered with old jute sacks or polythene sheets. The quantity of salt used is estimated to be 1:9 salt:fish. |
| Fermented | Salting takes one to seven days, during which time the product is fermented. |
| Dried | The fermented fish is then sun-dried on the ground for one to three days. |
| Product | A dry but soft and strongly flavoured product is obtained. Bomone is used for flavouring soups and stews. |

*Source:* Nerquaye-Tetteh, G. *et al.*, 1978

| Region | West Africa |
|---|---|
| Country | Ghana |
| Product | Salted-dried trigger fish |
| Local name | Ewura Efua |
| Raw material | Trigger fish (*Balistes capriscus*) |
| Prepared | Gutted and washed |
| Salted | Salt sprinkled on fish which are arranged in wooden or concrete troughs. The ratio of salt is estimated to be in the range of 1:3 — 1:6. The troughs are covered under shade for half a day to one day. |
| Dried | The fish is then spread out in the sun to dry completely. |
| Product | Very dry with tough skin which needs to be peeled off before the fish is used for preparing food. The salt content is sometimes high and the product needs to be de-salted before consumption by soaking in water. When well-dried, salted-dried trigger fish can be stored for some months. |

| Region | West Africa |
|---|---|
| Countries | Several |
| Product | Smoked dried fish |
| Local name | Smoked dried Bonga |
| Raw material | Fish (*Ethmalosa*) |
| Prepared | Washed |
| Cooked | The fish are laid whole on top of a bamboo rack in alternate layers with sticks until about five layers thick. The rack is supported on poles inside a smokehouse constructed of sticks and palm leaves. The fish are cooked for twelve hours over a hardwood fire. |
| Smoked | The fire is re-kindled and allowed to smoulder to smoke the fish for a following three to four days. During this time the fish are rearranged each day. The length of the smoking period depends on the product desired. |
| Dried | The fish are moved to a loft above the smokehouse and placed in an upright position (heads down) for seven days to dry in the hot air from the smokehouse. |
| Product | Dark colour, hard texture, heavily smoked and deformed. It has a long storage life if hard-dried, though half-dried bonga is also produced which has a short storage life. |

*Source:* FAO, 1970

| Region | Africa |
|---|---|
| Countries | The Gambia, Sierra Leone |
| Product | Smoked marine catfish |
| Local name | Kong, ngunja, catfish |
| Raw material | Catfish (*Arius*) |
| Prepared | Cut open ventrally to remove viscera. Any roe is kept separate. Soaked in boiling water and then scrubbed with lime to remove slime. |
| Smoked | The fish is drained and hot smoked on banda using coconut husk and/or wood. |
| Product | Golden brown smoked fish. |

*Note:* The roe, which are large and round, are washed with salt and lime and then boiled to produce a hard white yolky substance. When in season, they are sold as a snack. This same method can be used for riverine catfish (*Clarias sp*), which has great potential in aquaculture.

| Region | Africa |
|---|---|
| Countries | The Gambia, Senegal |
| Product | Fermented sun-dried fish |
| Local name | Gaedja |
| Raw material | Fish species preferably *Pseudotholitus* |
| Prepared | Fish is washed and split open dorsally, viscera is removed. |
| Sun-dried | The fish ferments while drying slowly over several days. |
| Product | Hard, sun-dried fish that can keep indefinitely if kept away from moisture. Used as a condiment. |

*Note:* The same technique is used for dry salted fish, adding salt before sun-drying. Gaedja is also eaten with Yate (fermented and sun-dried marine snail), which forms the basis of the national dish in The Gambia and Senegal.

| Region | Africa |
|---|---|
| Countries | The Gambia, Sierra Leone |
| Product | Wet salted fish |
| Raw material | Demersal species |
| Prepared | Fish is washed and scaled. Split open dorsally or cut up in steaks and split at the back bone. |
| Salted | Salt is ground/pounded to fine powder and applied liberally to fish, then stacked. Fish is then covered with jute sack. |
| Product | Wet salted fish can keep for months. |
| Marketing | This technique was extremely popular when trade between The Gambia (fish) and Sierra Leone (dry goods) was at its peak in the 1950s and 60s. With the spread of air travel and the withdrawal of passenger lines that sailed from Liverpool to Lagos via major West African ports, this trade has diminished. |

| Region | Africa |
|---|---|
| Country | Kenya, Tanzania, Uganda |
| Product | Smoked fish |
| Local name | Mbutu |
| Raw material | Nile perch (*Nates niloticus*) |
| Prepared | Scaled, gutted and split without washing. May be sold fresh or further processed by smoking or frying. |
| Fried/smoked | The cut pieces are placed on crude trays over an enclosed, rectangular mud oven. The fire is then lit inside the bottom of the oven. Alternatively, the fish may be fried in its own oil. |
| Market | The buyers (women) come to the site and buy fresh, fried or smoked fish to take to markets where the fish may be re-fried or smoked before selling. |

*Traditional 'lunyo'
rectangular
smoking oven
at Ragwe, Kenya*

| | |
|---|---|
| Region | East Africa |
| Countries | Tanzania, Kenya, Uganda |
| Product | Sun-dried fish |
| Local names | Kapenta (Zambia), Ndagaa (Tanzania), Omena (Kenya) |
| Raw material | Tilapia (*Limnothrissa*), anchovies (*Haplocromis*) |
| Prepared | Small fish left whole, large fish are split. |
| Sun-dried | Laid on the ground or on mats for several days. |
| Product | Dried fish |

| | |
|---|---|
| Region | North Africa |
| Country | Egypt |
| Product | Fermented fish |
| Local name | Fasikh |
| Raw material | Small pelagies |
| Salted (pickled) | Placed in large margarine-type tins in alternate layers of fish and salt. |
| Fermented | Left to ferment and topped up with fish and salt. |
| Product | Sold in the tins after the correct length of fermentation has taken place. |

| | |
|---|---|
| Region | South America |
| Country | Peru/Ecuador |
| Product | Salted fish |
| Local name | Salpreso |
| Raw material | Mullet/mackerel (*Scomber japonicus*) |
| Prepared | Gutted, dorsal split ('kippered') |

| Salted | 25–30% (wet weight) dry salt in dry (kench) pile. |
|---|---|
| Stacked | In open air/on stones until transported (several days to two weeks). |
| Product | Salpreso (salted fish). |
| Market | Andean towns/villages. |

| Region | South America |
|---|---|
| Country | Ecuador – Galapagos Islands |
| Product | Salted dried grouper |
| Local name | Bacalao |
| Raw material | Large groupers (e.g. *Myteroperca olfax*) |
| Prepared | Dorsally split, gutted and salted on fishing boats – kench piles in wooden boxes stored on deck. |
| Dried | On black lava (volcanic) rocks, roofs of houses, etc. |
| Packed | Jute/plastic woven sacks, shipped to mainland. |
| Market | Consumed during Lent/Easter and in 'fanesca' soups. |

| Region | South America |
|---|---|
| Country | Peru, Chile, Argentina |
| Product | Salted/fermented fish |
| Local name | Anchoa |
| Raw material | Anchovies (*Engraulis ringens*) |
| Prepared | Whole fresh fish mixed with 35 per cent dry salt in barrels. Wet pile (salt covers fish). Left for three to four months or more to mature (fermentation due to enzymes, giving strong odour and red colour). |
| Market | Local and northern hemisphere (pizzas), often canned in olive oil for luxury overseas market. |

| Region | South America |
|---|---|
| Country | Peru/Chile |
| Product | Fish marinated in citric acid |
| Local name | Ceviche |
| Raw material | Any fish/shellfish. Often sardine, bass, shark. |
| Prepared | Fresh fish is chopped into cubes/pieces about one or two centimetres. Lime juice is squeezed over cubes to cover and left to marinade for several hours. Often other ingredients are added, such as chilli or herbs. |
| Market | Local consumption |

| Region | South America |
|---|---|
| Country | Peru |
| Product | Dry-salted fish |
| Raw material | Hake/shark |
| Prepared | Head removed and gutted, cut along dorsal side. Two-thirds spinal column is removed. |
| Salted | Fish are salted adding 30 per cent salt concentration. Stacked in alternate salt and fish layers (kench pile). |
| Dried | Dried for five to six days, alternating in the shade and sun. |
| Packed | In jute sacks or polythene bags and put in wooden boxes. |
| Market | For export. At Easter, local consumption of dry-salted fish is traditional. |

*Source:* Reaño, 1986

| Region | South America |
|---|---|
| Country | Peru |
| Product | Dried fish |
| Local name | Dried Ishpis |
| Raw material | 'Ishpis' are small fish caught in lake Titicaca in the Peruvian highlands. |
| Dried | Left to dry whole in the sun near boats. The low relative humidity (45–60 per cent) of the area aids drying. |
| Product | Ishpis consumed locally. Because of the air drying, the product is highly oxidized. |

*Source:* Reaño, 1986

| Region | South-east Asia |
|---|---|
| Country | Indonesia |
| Product | Prawn/fish cracker |
| Local name | Keropok |
| Raw material | Good quality fish (sardine and dorad species are preferred) or prawns. |
| Prepared | The flesh of the fish is stripped from the bones (prawns are peeled), mixed with sago or tapioca flour by passing through a mincer, or pestle and mortar. Ratio of fish to flour varies, can be 1:1. Monosodium glutamate, salt, sugar, red colouring (optional) are added. |
| Pounded | Using pestle and mortar. |
| Rolled | The mixture is rolled into sausages when it begins to gel. |
| Cooked | In steam or boiling water until gelatinized. |

| | |
|---|---|
| Sliced | After cooling they are sliced into rounds about two millimetres thick. |
| Dried | Dried in the sun for about one day and then packed into polythene pouches for distribution. |
| Product | Snack food which can accompany more substantial meals. |

*Note:* The manufacture of Keropok is an important cottage industry, mostly carried out by women. This product is widespread throughout South-east Asia.

| | |
|---|---|
| Region | South-east Asia |
| Countries | Indonesia, Philippines, Japan |
| Product | Salted smoked fish |
| Local name | Salted smoked bandeng |
| Raw material | Milkfish |
| Prepared | Gutted, cleaned |
| Salted | Placed in salt solution (brine) (1½kg salt to 20kg fish) for two hours, then drained. |
| Spiced | Salt and spices are placed in the gut cavity. |
| Smoked | In vertical smokehouses for two to three hours. Fish are hung from frames. The fuel used is charcoal, sprinkled periodically with wood chips. |
| Storage | Stored for three days before distribution (ensures salt spice are absorbed into flesh). |

*Note:* This product is also found in the Philippines and Japan.
*Source:* FAO, 1970

| | |
|---|---|
| Region | South-east Asia |
| Country | Indonesia |
| Product | Salted boiled fish |
| Local name | Pindang |
| Raw material | Milkfish, sardines and herring. |
| Prepared | Washed, gutted and cut into pieces to fit inside pots or cans. |
| Salted | Placed inside earthenware or tin containers and layered alternately with salt (the concentration varies depending on desired storage life and taste of product). Water is added to fill the container. |
| Cooked | Container heated above a fire until fish is cooked. |
| Re-salted | Most of the water is drained away and more salt is added to the surface fish. |
| Cooked | Cooking continues until no free water remains in the container. |
| Storage | The container is sealed with leaves or paper and distributed. Storage life varies between a few days and a few months. |

*Source:* ILO, 1982

*Traditional layering
of salt and fish for the
production of Pindang*

*Traditional processing
of Pindang*

| Region | South-east Asia |
| --- | --- |
| Country | Indonesia |
| Product | Salted dried fish |
| Local name | Jambal |
| Raw material | Marine catfish |
| Prepared | Heads and guts removed. Submerged in water for twenty-four hours (some fermentation occurs). Removed from water. |
| Salted | Pickle salted, using solar salt, for twenty-four hours. |
| Dried | Sun-dried for three to six days. |
| Packaging | Sometimes packed in polythene bags. |

| | |
|---|---|
| Region | South-east Asia |
| Country | Philippines |
| Product | Salted smoked fish |
| Local name | Tinapa |
| Raw material | Sardines, milkfish |
| Prepared | Washed; large fish are gutted. |
| Salted | Soaked in saturated brine solution in large tub. The soaking time depends on the size of the fish used. |
| Cooked | Fish are placed in baskets made of wood or bamboo strips and suspended in iron kettles or boilers until cooked. |
| Dried | In the baskets and left to cool (usually overnight). |
| Smoked | Arranged in smoking trays inside a furnace heated with charcoal and sawdust. Smoking times vary depending on size of fish and the taste desired. The position of the trays is alternated to provide as even a cure as possible. |
| Marketed | Cooled and packaged in coarse woven rattan baskets. Storage time from three to seven days at ambient temperatures. |

*Source:* FAO, 1970

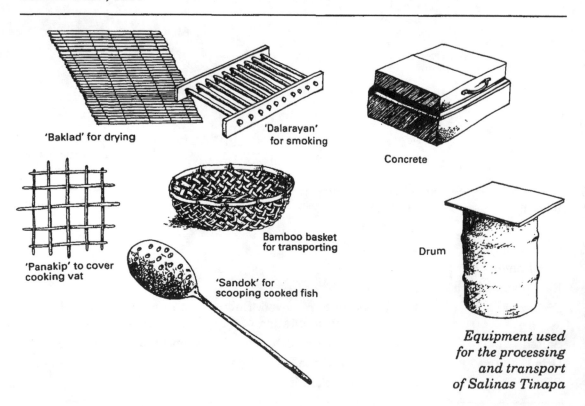

'Baklad' for drying

'Dalarayan' for smoking

Concrete

'Panakip' to cover cooking vat

Bamboo basket for transporting

'Sandok' for scooping cooked fish

Drum

*Equipment used for the processing and transport of Salinas Tinapa*

| Region | South-east Asia |
|---|---|
| Country | Philippines |
| Product | Boiled smoked fish |
| Local name | Tinapa Salinas method |
| Raw material | Roundscad, milkfish, sardines, mackerel |
| Prepared | Washed |
| Sun-dried | For two hours. |
| Boiled | Cooked in saturated boiling brine until the eyes turn white. |
| Smoked | Sprinkled with water to remove scum and drained before smoking for thirty to forty five minutes. The smoking kilns used are completely closed except for the opening at the top where the smoking trays are placed. |
| Product | Tinapa cooled and packed in baskets covered with banana leaves. |

*Source:* Bulaong *et al.*, 1986

| Region | East Asia |
|---|---|
| Country | Japan |
| Product | Smoked dried fish |
| Local name | Katsuobushi |
| Raw material | Tuna |
| Prepared | Head, guts and fins removed. Washed, filleted and cut into strips. Vertebral column removed. |
| Steamed | Arranged in shallow flat baskets suspended in kettle above boiling water for forty to sixty minutes, until cooked. |
| Cooled | Once cool, the fish are dipped into tub of water and the skin stripped off to remove fat, ribs and spines. Bones carefully removed. |
| Smoked | Placed on flat basket and suspended in smoke oven and turned once. Smoked for thirty minutes on each side. |
| Moulded | Fish flesh previously discarded is kneaded into damaged parts and smoothed down. |
| Smoked | Forty minutes smoking repeated six to ten times, during which the temperature is reduced. |
| Sun-dried | For three to four days. Surface scraped and remoulded as before followed by two more days of sun drying. |
| Stored | In boxes for two weeks to produce a mould on fish surface. |
| Sun-dried | One to two days after which the storing and drying process, to allow for mould growth, is repeated four to five times. |
| Product | Storage life is almost indefinite, providing each month the product is re-dried in the sun for a day. Eaten as shavings which are scraped off to flavour soups etc. |

*Source:* FAO, 1970

| | |
|---|---|
| Region | South-east Asia |
| Country | Philippines |
| Product | Fermented fish |
| Local name | Bagoong |
| Raw material | Anchovy, sardines. |
| Prepared | Washed in clean water. |
| Salted | Placed in concrete or wooden vat and mixed with salt in a ratio of 3:1, fish to salt. |
| Fermented | Salt and fish mixture is transferred to earthenware jars or oil drums and covered with cheesecloth for five days and then sealed. They are left in the sun for seven days before transferring the product to five gallon cans. These cans are left to stand for three to twelve months to allow further fermentation of the product. |
| Product | 'Bagoong' has a paste-like consistency and reddish colour. It can be stored for many years. |

*Source:* ILO, 1982

| | |
|---|---|
| Region | South-east Asia |
| Country | Burma |
| Product | Fermented fish |
| Local name | Ngapi |
| Raw material | Small anchovies |
| Prepared | Washed in sea water. |
| Dried | In the sun for two days. |
| Salted | One part salt is added to six parts dried fish in a bamboo basket. |
| Pounded | To form a paste which is then packed into wooden tubs or boxes to remove all air bubbles. |
| Fermented | The paste is left to ferment for seven days. |
| Pounded and salted | For approximately three hours, while adding the same amount of salt as previously added. |
| Dried | Spread in the sun for three to five hours. |
| Fermented | Left to continue fermenting in wooden tubs, for one month, then pounded once more. |
| Product | 'Ngapi' has a pasty consistency and can be stored for two years in anaerobic conditions, contained in tubs or earthenware pots. Sometimes artificial dyes (which can be toxic) are added to improve colour. |

*Source:* ILO, 1982

| Region | South-east Asia |
|---|---|
| Country | Vietnam |
| Product | Fermented fish sauce |
| Local name | Nuoc-mam |
| Raw material | Anchovy, scads |
| Prepared | Washed and kneaded by hand before mixing with salt. |
| Salted | One part salt is added to three parts fish in earthenware pots. |
| Fermented | The pots are buried in the ground for a few months. |
| Product | Nuoc-mam is a clear liquid which rises to the top of the fermented product and is filtered off. The residue is used as a fertilizer. |

*Source:* ILO, 1982

| Region | South-east Asia |
|---|---|
| Country | Philippines |
| Product | Lactic fermented fish |
| Local name | Burong-isda |
| Raw material | Shrimp, milkfish, silver perch, mudfish, catfish, gourami, tilapia. |
| Prepared | Scaled, gutted, washed and drained. |
| Salted | 10–30 per cent salt concentration for two to six hours, after which the fish is removed from the brine that develops. |
| Mixed | With boiled rice in the ratio three to five parts rice to one part fish. Ginger and garlic may be added. |
| Fermented | Fish and rice are packed together in a jar and left for one to two weeks before consumption. |
| Product | Burong-isda is sautéd with garlic and onion and eaten with vegetables. |

*Source:* Adams *et al.*, 1985

| Region | South-east Asia |
|---|---|
| Country | Philippines |
| Product | Lactic fermented fish |
| Local name | Balao-balao |
| Raw material | Shrimp |
| Prepared | The antennae of the live shrimps are removed. Washed and drained. |
| Salted | Placed in 15–20 per cent salt concentration and left to stand for three to six hours before draining. |

| | |
|---|---|
| Mixed | With salted boiled rice. The shrimp:rice:salt ratio is 1:4.8:0.2 |
| Fermented | Packed in jars and left to ferment for seven to ten days. |
| Product | Sautéd in oil with garlic and onion before serving. |

*Source:* Adams *et al.*, 1985

| | |
|---|---|
| Region | Asia |
| Country | South India |
| Product | Fermented fish |
| Local name | Colombo cure |
| Raw material | Mackerel, non-fatty sardines |
| Prepared | Gutted, gilled and washed in sea water. |
| Salted | Mixed with dry salt, (one part salt to three parts fish), in concrete tanks. The dried fruit pulp of tamarind is added to the salt and fish to increase the acidity level of the mixture. |
| Fermented | Fish are weighed down in the brine mixture with stones on mats and left for two to four months. They are then transferred to wooden barrels, packed tightly and kept topped up with pickling solution. |
| Product | 'Colombo cure' is the whole fermented fish, which has a fruity odour and firm but flaky flesh and can be stored for over a year. The remaining pickle is used as a fish sauce. |

*Source:* ILO, 1982

# Prevention of insect infestation

Traditional methods used to deter insects are virtually unrecorded. It has been observed that local village fish processors in The Gambia use chilli sprinkled over the fish while it is drying to prevent blowfly infestation and similarly lime juice is used by Senegalese fish processors. In Malawi, sand is applied to the fish to deter blowflies. However, this may introduce bacteria.

The only reference to a traditional method of preventing beetle infestation is in Mali where the local processors scatter pepper in a ring around fish placed in bundles or, alternatively, the powdered leaves of *Bosia Senegalensis* may be used (NRI, private communication).

Recent experimental work at Imperial College, UK, has shown that dried citrus peel, powdered and added to dried fish prevents beetle infestation.

During the wet season, when blowfly infestation is at its peak and fish losses are high, the most effective traditional method of insect control, used some fifty years ago by the fishermen, was not to fish at all.

Fish processors realized that climatic conditions (high relative humidities in particular) were unfavourable for sun-drying and hence for the keeping quality of fish. However, in view of the shortage of protein-rich foods, and the consequent pressure put on fisheries to increase the total catch, this effective , traditional preventive measure is not often used today (NRI, private communication).

# 3
# Improved processing and equipment

WHEN TALKING OF 'improved' fish processing techniques, care must be taken about how the term is applied. Traditional methods have evolved over hundreds of years and are continuing to evolve. In many cases traditional methods are still the best way of processing fish for local markets.

Traditional methods only break down when factors impinging on these activities change at a faster rate than traditional technical adaptations. These external factors could include a number of things such as introduced species, a worsening shortage of a convenient and/or inexpensive fuel, depletion of stocks through over-fishing or the changing consumer habits of urban populations.

It is in these cases that improvements can probably be effectively introduced. Whoever is introducing any such improvements, however, must aim to involve the processing community fully in any process of innovation, since they will understand much better than any outsider just what will and will not work. The advisor must also have active experience of both traditional and improved techniques and equipment in order to be able to appreciate the merits and limitations of different methods. Economic considerations need to be assessed too. While a piece of equipment might at first seem to have a good rate of return, the sheer scarcity of capital may mean that a 'cheap' piece of equipment to an outsider may be beyond any possible risk that a fish processor could take.

This section looks at improved techniques and equipment that have been tried out. It follows the same pattern as

the previous chapters. You are urged to follow the checklist in Chapter 5 and the principles in Chapter 2 before attempting any introduction of improved technology.

The health and safety aspects of any process must not be overlooked. Because fish is a low-acid food, careful and rapid processing following the correct procedures is essential. For example, if insufficient salt is used during salting, or if the conditions produced through reducing fermentation times cause acidic levels which are too low, then the growth of pathogens such as *Clostridium botulinum* may be lethal. This bacterium produces botulinum toxin under certain conditions and is responsible for the condition known as botulism which has a 70 per cent lethality rate in man. Care must be taken to ensure that people receive correct health and safety training, especially where a new product or process is being introduced.

## Pre-processing aspects

### Effective handling practices

It has been mentioned in Chapter 2 that the quality of raw fish available to the processor depends on the way it has been handled from the point of catch. In general, the processor will have little direct control over the way that fishermen capture, handle, prepare and store fish on their boats. However, when fish supplies are plentiful, the merchants can place a demand for high quality raw material. Consultants should be aware of these aspects and seek ways of improving the quality of the fish available to processors by liaison with local fisheries specialists.

As soon as a fish dies, spoilage begins. The ideal way to keep a fish fresh is to keep it alive until processed. However that may be very difficult to achieve.

If, as is more common, the fish dies after it is caught it should ideally be bled, gutted and gilled before landing, providing the methods used are correct and hygienic. However, if fish are sold by weight, fishermen may be reluctant to do this. Hygiene on board the fishing vessel is important; knives need to be cleaned, gutting areas washed down and guts thrown away.

To help maintain freshness the catch should be stored in cool, shady areas. The extent to which the fish have been bruised by rough handling, being trodden on, thrown about and moved by using shovels will also have an effect on their freshness.

The importance of good hygiene continues after landing and here good practices come under the control of the processors. Fish landing sites and processing areas should be kept as clean as possible, waste being removed and disposed of so as not to attract insects and vermin. Unhygienic and insanitary conditions attract blowflies in particular. Fish should be prepared for processing off the ground, preferably on a clean surface. Plastic and metal surfaces are considerably easier to keep clean than wooden ones. If possible processing areas should have access to clean water so that knives, tables etc. can be regularly cleaned. If no water of drinking quality is available, a small amount of household bleach in water will greatly assist in maintaining the cleanliness of tables and implements. Fish, before and after processing, should be kept cool and covered to avoid flies landing on them and laying their eggs. Caution needs to be used particularly when large catches are landed during sea-sonal gluts, when the time interval between landing and processing fish is increased.

## Maintaining fish at low temperatures

The rate of microbiological and chemical deterioration that takes place after the death of a fish is temperature-dependent and typical tropical temperatures will accelerate spoilage. Any measures taken to reduce the temperature of the catch by keeping it in the shade, covering with wet sacks or ice will play a significant role in maintaining quality.

Whether the fish are on water or on land, the best way to keep them cool (without sophisticated refrigeration facilities) is with ice. However, in many areas ice may not be available and fish can then be kept relatively cool by other means, including the following:

o keeping the fish in the shade out of direct sun

o evaporative cooling — i.e. placing clean damp sacking over the fish. This helps reduce the temperature as the water evaporates. The sacking must be kept wet and clean and the fish must be well ventilated. This can be done by laying small sticks across the containers under the sacking or mixing the fish with wet grass or water weeds in an open-sided box so that the water can evaporate and cool the fish. The fish should be kept continuously wet (see page 54).

Fish will generally only keep a few hours, however, unless ice is used.

## The use of ice

The use of ice can significantly increase the shelf-life of fresh fish both at sea after capture and handling ashore. The water used in ice-making should be reasonably clean and sea water or brackish water can be used, although there are disadvantages in using sea water.

Ice should be mixed with the fish using a fish-to-ice ratio adequate to keep the fish at low enough temperature until processing or sale. Often, especially during transport, insulated containers are necessary to prevent the ice from melting too fast. Therefore, with the use of ice comes the use of appropriate containers, and this may represent a substantial investment. However, it has been suggested that the cost of ice is the limiting factor for icing fish in tropical countries rather than the cost of the containers (Lupin, 1985). In addition, ice represents a continuing operational cost.

It is probably not widely recognized that in tropical countries, not only is ice often unavailable but its relative cost compared to the other costs involved in fresh fish handling is so high that its use in small-scale fisheries is entirely inappropriate, unless changes are made in organization, capital investment and infrastructure. This is reflected in the fact that the final cost of the use of ice for fresh fish could be as much as twenty times higher in tropical and subtropical countries than in temperate and cold countries (Lupin, 1985). Further to these economic constraints are the physical limitations such as the ice melting more quickly in the higher tropical temperatures; the availability of appropriate containers and the loss of space during transportation and storage.

Perhaps the final, major, point to raise is that it is a waste of time using ice if not enough of it is used. The fish-to-ice ratio represents a mixture of the two in proportions adequate to keep the fish cool enough for the required distribution or storage time. The most suitable containers are those which provide adequate insulation to reduce the melting rate of ice. Another problem is that small vessels used in artisanal fishing often do not have the capacity for ice containers.

If the use of ice is to be considered as a fish preservation technique then careful planning and organization are essential. The cost of installing ice facilities (to provide ice continuously and at the required production levels), and the existence of suitable infrastructure must be carefully assessed, along with the existing markets for fresh and processed fish and likely consumer acceptance. It is not uncommon to find resistance to icing, as the consumer may believe that the reason why the fish is iced is because it is poor quality. Research institutes, such as NRI and FAO have carried out much work in this area and have gained valuable experience.

# Drying

The heat of the sun and the removal of moisture by movement of air (air speed) are the major factors which cause fish to dry, and these can be utilized to their full advantage by very simple changes in processing. It is more difficult to have any control over relative humidity, except by raising the air temperature.

In general, the optimal drying conditions for tropical fish species appear to be quite well established (FAO, 1981).

## Shade drying

In some cases fish can dry too quickly when exposed to both high temperature and strong wind, which can lead to case hardening.

To minimize this, fish can be initially dried in the shade. During the initial stage, careful drying is necessary at these shade temperatures. Thereafter, when the water is being removed from the fish interior, higher temperatures can be applied by moving the fish out of the shade. This reduces the drying time, allowing for a more efficient process.

## Drying racks

Drying fish directly on the ground or at ground level on mats or rocks has many disadvantages, and the use of raised drying racks (Figure 7) may offer substantial improvements because:

o air flow is increased at a metre or so above the ground;
o a greater surface area of the fish is exposed to air currents and temperatures;
o the fish is less accessible to predators;
o if the racks are sloping, any excess moisture can drain away;
o fish can be protected from water when it rains by covering with waterproof material. This is not possible if the fish are laid directly on the ground, as the underside of the fish will still be in contact with water;
o choosing a drying site where the wind is strong (i.e. increasing air flow) will aid drying (Clucas, 1982).

The same principles apply to drying ropes or poles, which are stretched between uprights on a beach or an open, windy area. The fish are then hung or draped on the ropes.

A constraint to the introduction of drying racks may be the additional costs incurred in their construction, which may not be realized in terms of the processing time saved or increased prices for the improved product.

## Drying platforms

Simple concrete or hard packed clay/earth drying platforms may offer the best alternative to simple drying on the ground.

These retain thermal energy and if kept clean can be very effective at drying. They are easy and cheap to construct.

## Solar drying

There has been a good deal of interest and research in recent years concerned with the development of a variety of solar driers as an improved method of drying fish in developing countries.

Researchers have found that by achieving regular increased drying temperatures and reducing humidities, solar driers can increase drying rates, and produce a lower moisture content in the final products, with resultant improvements in fish quality when compared with traditional sun drying techniques.

It has further been suggested that solar driers may offer some protection against adverse weather conditions, for example in wet seasons, and against attack by blowflies, beetles and other vermin. Temperatures in excess of 45°C may be attained inside solar driers, thereby killing insect pests.

The solar driers evaluated in the field have included:

o solar tent driers
o solar cabinet driers
o solar dome drier
o solar drier with separate collector and drying chamber.

Information on the principal operating features of these driers together with the basic theories of solar drying is reported in Trim and Curran, 1983; Brenndorfer *et al.*, 1985; and Curran *et al.*, 1985. Although solar drying relies on natural convection and so additional fuel costs are spared, the initial cost of construction materials and their replacement costs when they wear out need to be considered. The majority of the available designs are not particularly robust (e.g. in high winds), and may achieve temperatures which are too high, giving high initial drying rates causing fragmentation, case hardening or cooking effects, which all reduce product quality. Solar driers often have a fairly low capacity and the time needed for their construction may make them unattractive to artisans. Additionally, training must be given to educate local processors in the correct operation of the drier; for example, ensuring air vents are operated correctly to optimize ventilation.

To increase their capacity for holding fish, larger solar driers, such as the solar dome type, have been evaluated (Curran et al., 1985; Bostock et al., 1985). However, problems of inefficient drying rates and blowfly infestation have been encountered when using this drier in adverse weather conditions. The effectiveness of natural convection solar driers in reducing losses due to blowfly infestation is disputed.

Some researchers have had success in controlling blowfly infestation in fish using solar driers, whereas other workers have found that the insects become trapped inside. It is difficult to keep them from entering, and increasing the temperatures inside the drier sufficient to kill the blowflies reduces product quality (Walker, unpublished information; Curran et al., 1985). There is no evidence that these driers are used by artisanal fish processors, the main problem being the large capital investment in the face of competition from other producers.

## Artificial driers

In an attempt to address the problems posed by the difficulties of sun-drying in developing countries during the rainy season, when traditional drying may be impossible, various designs of artificial driers typically fuelled by agro-wastes, e.g. rice husk, have been tested. Such designs also have the potential of affording more control over temperature and air flow and thus over the drying process.

The high capital and maintenance costs of these artificial driers compared with traditional techniques, and the additional skills and training required for their operation may make them unsuitable or difficult to justify for general use with small-scale fish processors.

The following are examples of artificial driers:

o canvas drier
o tray drier
o IRRI fish drier
o low-cost fish drier (LCF)
o UPLB-IDRC drier
o SAM drier
o Steel drier.

The last five of these fish driers are prototypes resulting from extensive research carried out at the Universities of Los Baños and Visayas in the Philippines, together with various collaborators. The IRRI (International Rice Research Institute) drier was a joint effort between IRRI and Filipino-German Fisheries Project; the steel drier was also conceived under the Filipino-German Fisheries Project, and the UPLB-IDRC drier was a collaborative project between University of Los Baños and IRRI.

All of these prototype driers differ in their fuel use, construction materials, energy conversion, method of holding fish (hanging or placing on trays) and the design of the drying chamber and chimney. Further information on their construction and operation can be obtained from IRRI, IDRC or the universities in the Philippines (see Contacts list).

The IRRI drier has a unique Vortex Wind machine facility to harness wind energy, while the tray and the SAM (Solar Agro-waste Multipurpose) driers make use of solar energy and can be converted to artificial use when rain threatens.

A great deal of laboratory research has been carried out to test these driers (Jeon *et al.*, 1986; Roberts, 1986. Sison *et al.*, 1983; Villason and Flores, 1983; Orejana and Embuscado, 1983), but it appears that their use has not been tested significantly in the field and their advantages and disadvantages for use by small-scale processors are therefore unclear.

# Salting

Improved salting involves the application of processing techniques as described in Chapter 1 and the use of equipment does not therefore feature very strongly.

## Proper use of salt

Although preserving by salting has long been practised as a traditional technique, the ratios of salt to fish used are often too low to ensure adequate preservation. This may be because of constraints in availability and the cost of salt in particular locations, lack of adequate knowledge in salting techniques, or simply consumer preference. Attention should be drawn, however, to possible health hazards caused by inadequate processing. There have been outbreaks of lethal botulism from the growth of *Clostridium botulinum* on fish when insufficient salt has been used, for example, in the preparation of Pindang.

When the correct amounts of salt are used, this is an extremely effective way of preserving fish. Recommended levels of salt usage are 30–40 per cent of the prepared weight of fish. The use of more salt will not improve the process and simply adds to the production costs unnecessarily. Other considerations in salting are the size

and type of the salt crystals used. In dry salting, the FAO recommends the proportion of small to large crystals should be 1 to 2 respectively. In both wet and dry methods, the salt must be as clean as possible, as impurities in the salt affect its penetration rate into the fish flesh.

It is acknowledged, however, that it may be very difficult to obtain good quality salt; salt may not be available in different particle sizes and so whatever salt is available will have to be used.

## Brining

Brining differs from wet and dry salting in that the fish are immersed into a pre-prepared solution of salt (brine). Brining will not preserve the fish unless the correct strengths are used.

The brine is prepared by dissolving crystalline salt in water until no more salt will dissolve. This is termed a saturated solution or 100 per cent brine, and contains approximately 360g of salt per litre of water.

When the fish are added, there is an exchange of salt from the brine to the fish and water from the fish to the brine so diluting the strength of the brine. Thus it is necessary to check the strength of the brine periodically. Brine strength can be ensured by hanging a sack of salt in the solution, ensuring the brine remains saturated.

If the quality of available salt or water is poor, the brine could be boiled thoroughly, and any foam on the surface skimmed off. The brine is then allowed to cool before use. Another way is to bake the salt before making the brine.

The main advantage of brining is that it allows a more uniform cure, and by varying the concentration of the brine and the period of immersion, or curing period, it is possible to control the salt concentration in the final product.

A 10° brine, for example, which is made up by mixing one part of saturated (or 100°) brine with nine parts water is sometimes used to soak fish before dry salting. Brining is not generally used as a preservation method in itself but can be advantageously used as a preparatory treatment prior to further salting, smoking or drying.

## Brining and pressing

An experimental process involving a combination of brining and pressing has been described by Parry (Reilly and Bartile, 1986) which seems to have potential.

Briefly, fish are beheaded, eviscerated and washed, before being immersed in a saturated brine solution in a weighted, closely covered container. The mixture of fish and brine should be stirred and the brine checked daily to ensure it is saturated.

The rapid uptake of salt by the fish ensures microbiological safety and prevents spoilage. The fish remain in the saturated brine until the fish flesh is saturated with salt. This can take up to six days. Following brining the fish are packed in layers in a slatted wooden box and pressed for a period of between eight and eighteen hours; to remove excess moisture and air spaces between the fish which would encourage rancidity.

The salted fish form a compact block, and if packed in a polythene-lined carton, have a storage life of at least ten weeks. This method is experimental and has only been used so far with small pelagic species such as sardines.

An improved salting method now used in Peru consists of mixing dry salt (at a concentration of 30 per cent wet weight) with small pelagic, gutted fish in a wet pile. Pressing can be carried out if required, otherwise the fish are simply left in the brine pickle.

This will also impede oxidated rancidity. The storage life of the product is two to three months. Maturing reactions due to fermentation will become evident later (reddening of flesh and fruity odours).

This product is consumed mainly by the Andean Indian population (Bostock *et al.*, 1986).

# Smoking

The disadvantages of traditional smoking techniques and equipment have previously been mentioned in this section. In order to improve smoking techniques some control must be exercised over temperature, air flow and smoke density. Traditional open-type ovens produce non-uniform smoked products because of fluctuations in these factors. It is difficult for fish processors to improve their smoking techniques using traditional oven designs, particularly the pit type. One way is to pre-dry or salt the fish so that its moisture content is reduced before smoking. In order that more control over the smoking process can be exercised, attention has been paid to the development of improved smoking ovens. These have focused on aspects such as:

o increased fuel efficiency
o improvements in product quality and storage life
o provision of increased control over the smoking process to produce a standardized product
o increased durability of kilns
o achieving uniform smoke density
o better handling
o better ventilation system.

Efforts to improve smoking kilns, unlike improved drier design, have in general been more successful and have been introduced to small-scale fish processors.

Some improved kiln designs are:

o  Mud and pole kiln
o  Oil drum smoker
o  Watanabe fish smoker
o  Altona-type oven
o  Adjetey oven
o  Ivory Coast kiln
o  Chorkor
o  Innes Walker smoker.

Again, despite the merits of improved ovens, many new designs have not made any significant impact with artisanal fish processors. This is particularly true of the Altona-type oven and its variations. Although this closed kiln has, compared with the traditional pit type, an increased capacity, increased fuel efficiency and better control over temperature and smoke volume, its high initial cost and inappropriate building materials (cement, metal) are significant factors affecting its use. Interestingly, a version of the Altona-type used in the Tombo project, Sierra Leone, made operators skilled in loading traditional bandas redundant (Beck and During, 1986). Studies in a coastal village in The Gambia (NRI, private communication) showed that in order to keep up production levels of 11 tonnes of traditionally dried fish a day, 120 Altona ovens operating at capacities used in Nigeria (250 kilos fresh fish per day) would be needed. Traditionally the fish are stacked vertically along the bandas measuring forty feet in length by six feet wide and in this

**Table 3. Summary of the technical performance of different types of smoking ovens**

| Oven type | Species smoked | Weight fish smoked (kg) | Weight fuel used (kg) | Weight fuel/ fresh fish (kg) | Weight fuel/ smoked fish (kg, adjusted) | Process time (hrs) |
|---|---|---|---|---|---|---|
| Chorkor, mud | Tuna | 226 | 49.3 | 0.21 | 0.26 | 4.15 |
| | Sardinella | 180 | 63.6 | 0.35 | 0.42 | 7.40 |
| Chorkor, brick | Tuna | 230 | 56.5 | 0.24 | 0.35 | 3.40 |
| | Sardinella | 224 | 65.8 | 0.29 | 0.51 | 8.00 |
| Oil drum | Tuna | 71 | 20.9 | 0.29 | 0.28 | 3.00 |
| | Sardinella | 38 | 22.4 | 0.6 | 1.17 | 7.30 |
| Traditional mud | Tuna | 61 | 25.1 | 0.39 | 0.59 | 3.10 |
| | Sardinella | 331 | 21.2 | 0.92 | 1.58 | 7.60 |
| Altona | Tuna | 182 | 40.1 | 0.22 | 0.28 | 4.30 |
| | Sardinella | 184 | 36.5 | 0.7 | 1.13 | 7.00 |
| Ivory Coast | Tuna | 130 | 45.4 | 0.35 | 0.46 | 4.45 |
| | Sardinella | 76 | 35.9 | 0.47 | 0.81 | 7.00 |
| Pit oven | Tuna | 3.4 | 4.7 | 1.38 | 1.96 | 1.00 |
| | Sardinella | 2.7 | 7.4 | 2.7 | 4.7 | 5.00 |

Source: Stroud, G.D., 1986

way a large quantity is smoked. The construction and operation costs of Altona ovens compared to traditional bandas would be very unattractive to the artisans.

The construction of the Chorkor or Kagan smoker has been reviewed by Brownhill, 1983. Since its first introduction to West Africa, the Chorkor smoker has proved very popular with the local women processors, who produce a better quality product. It has naturally had some disadvantages, however, such as:

o frequent necessary replacement of netting on trays
o recent unavailability of wire netting for fish trays
o reduced 'chimney effect' because of difficulties in operating a large number of trays
o cracking of mud oven base due to higher temperatures reached
o burning of the sides of the trays
o not enough depth in the trays.

The Chorkor oven has been introduced to other countries in West Africa (see case study in Chapter 4).

Other methods introduced to improve smoking ovens have generally included the installation of a smoke spreader to control smoke density; more shelves to increase capacity; separate fire box, smoke accumulators and smoking chamber; and construction allowing for portability and batch handling.

Tables 3 and 4 give a comparison of the technical performance of different types of traditional and improved smoking ovens.

## Fermentation

Because of the nature of fermentation, where enzymatic activity is effectively part of the process, there has been little need for improved fermentation techniques for small-scale production. For larger-scale production there have been improvements in accelerating the rate of fermentation, but these are not applicable to artisanal processors.

## Prevention of insect infestation

There are many simple, inexpensive and appropriate ways to reduce insect attack by improving processing techniques: for example, improving salting, smoking and drying techniques in the ways which have been mentioned earlier. Some blowflies are able to develop a salt tolerance; for example, in West Java, blowflies will reproduce and feed off fish in a pickling solution of high salt concentration. A salt level as high as 35 per cent (salt content in processed fish) is needed before blowflies are inhibited. This may give an unacceptably salty product.

Probably one of the most notable improvements aimed at inhibiting insect infestation is the use of insecticides, which deserves mention here because of the high demand for them and their widespread use. However, their use should be regarded as a last resort and improved processing techniques must be considered first.

The first field application of an insecticide to protect fish was carried out in Chad in 1956. Since then, use of insecticides has escalated to a degree that warrants concern over the potential hazards of their indiscriminate use. Because blowflies and beetles can be killed by any insecticide, it is easy for people to purchase locally any cheap insecticide perhaps not even of food grade quality (i.e. those specifically for cash crops, large animals or household use). This is not only a problem for local fish processors but also for fish

**Table 4.  Summary of features of different smoking ovens**

| Oven type | Fuel use | Construction cost | Ease of operation | Control of smoking and drying | Useful life |
|---|---|---|---|---|---|
| Chorkor, mud | Good | Low | Good; well accepted by smokers | By rearrangement of trays | Short, unless covered and well maintained |
| Chorkor, brick | Good; less efficient than mud Chorkor | Moderate | As above | As above | Long, but some bricks showing signs of cracking |
| Oil drum | Tuna – good Sardinella – fair | High | Poor; disliked by smokers, who have to work over a smoking fire | Difficult, fire must be removed to rearrange fish | Medium, tends to rust |
| Traditional mud | Poor | Low | Poor, as above | Difficult, as above | Short, unless covered and maintained |
| Altona | Tuna – good Sardinella – fair | Very high | Poor; awkward to load, highest trays, disliked by smokers | By arranging trays | Long |
| Ivory Coast | Moderate | High | Moderate; could be improved by providing tray handles | As above | Moderate |
| Pit oven | Poor | Low | Good | By rearranging fish | Short |

*Source:* Stroud, G.D., 1986

| Potential for storage of smoked product | Quality of product | Temperature distribution | Transportable | Capacity |
|---|---|---|---|---|
| Good | Good | Variable, dependent on wind strength | No | High |
| Good | Good | As above | No | High |
| Moderate | Medium; tends to burn fish in centre of oven; fish marked | Variable; high centre temperature, poor insulation | Yes | Moderate |
| Moderate | Good; even drying and good colour; fish marked | Good | No | Moderate |
| Poor | Good, but surface of product inadequately dried | Vertical distribution good; horizontal distribution variable | No | Moderate |
| Good | Medium; smoke tends to condense on spreader plate; poor colour of smoked product | Vertical distribution good; horizontal distribution variable | Possible | High |
| Not possible | Good | Variable | No | Low |

technologists playing an advisory role, who may have no background in entomology (the study of insects). For any application of insecticides, specialist advice should be sought.

If the use of chemicals is to be continually abused (it has been observed that fish processors use DDT, petrol, kerosene and others to combat infestation), then the availability and cost of an insecticide which is safe and easy to use on fish for consumption, could help prevent hazardous consequences of using non-food grade insecticides.

One such product is pirimiphos-methyl (sold under the trade name *Actellic*), given clearance by WHO and FAO in November 1985 to be used on fish. It is one of the safest food-grade insecticides and is available at a cost similar to that of insecticides already in frequent use. Its effectiveness depends on its application and again, specialist advice should be sought. Trials carried out by NRI in Africa have shown that the effectiveness of *Actellic* depends on the size and oil content of fish, because these factors affect penetration rates and concentration uniformity.

# 4
# Case studies

WOMEN PLAY A vital role in traditional fish processing and marketing. Their efforts have been largely taken for granted and their needs ignored. This may be because opportunity to voice their needs has not arisen, or because someone else has answered for them. Furthermore, with only limited funds to allocate for development, governments usually place priority on those steps which will produce immediate gains, such as adding outboard motors to traditional fishing canoes to increase fish catches. Improving smoking ovens or fish driers provides far less obvious results. Yet without improvements in traditional processing methods, women continue to slip behind their male counterparts, who fish with modern motors and work in the few modern canning factories. Moreover, increased yields of fish are wasted because the processors are unable to keep pace with the supply (ECA, 1984).

It is often assumed that because women have been processing fish for centuries, they are naturally conservative or antagonistic to new ideas or devices. They are naturally mistrustful of new ideas being brought in by outsiders (after all 'development ideas' do not have a very good record) but when they can see clear benefits for themselves they are likely to want to adopt them.

The failure of introduced ideas in these circumstances is much more likely to be in the design of the project than in any innate conservatism. Often, the key constraint facing the women, as perceived by themselves, has not been central to a project. For example, in Togo, the problems affecting processors are a shortage of fish rather than firewood, of underemployment rather than lack of capacity (see case study).

Secondly, assumptions are made about the willingness of people to organize co-operatively. When no tradition of organization exists, establishing co-operatives can often lead to recriminations, mistrust and, ultimately, collapse. The Sierra Leone case study amply shows this.

Thirdly, while schemes are shown to be 'economic', no realistic attempt is made to ensure that the improvements are affordable. In many pilot projects, the equipment is given to the beneficiaries and no credit systems are established to enable other groups of women to take up the technology. This accounts for why, in Guinea, the Chorkor smokers have been taken up by private male entrepreneurs, leaving the women out altogether.

Fourthly, pilot projects often fail in establishing adequate extension programmes to ensure that other women have access to the technology. Such activities include sensibilization (creating awareness and motivating people to participate), training of artisans and fish processors in all relevant skills, follow-up support and adequate market research where new products are being introduced. The lack of these facilities has led, for example, to the down-grading of the Chorkor technology in Ghana, where untrained artisans have built substandard smokers.

There is potential for introducing improvements. The Chorkor smoker proves that, but improvements can only be introduced by involving the women themselves and enabling them to elaborate the social, cultural and economic content of any fish processing activity. Furthermore, design adaptation should be allowed to take place in order to fit in more closely with the women's own priorities and capacities.

Lastly, and probably most important of all, small changes often bring about the greatest benefits because they initiate a process of development. Large changes often have the effect of removing a process from the hands of those the improvements were designed to help. Project planners should never forget that.

---

# Chorkor smoker – Nyanyano, Ghana

---

The Chorkor smoker was originally developed in 1969–71 by the women of Chorkor, Ghana, FAO, and the Food Research Institute, Accra.

The Chorkor smoker has gained wide acceptance in the area with traditional processors and has been popular for the following reasons:

o low cost of construction;
o working life of four to fifteen years depending upon the strength of materials used for construction;
o a smoking capacity of up to 18kg of fish per tray;
o low consumpton of fuelwood and higher retention of heat leading to a better quality product;
o reduction in labour time.

The Chorkor smoker was designed specifically to address the following problems in traditional processing methods:

o poor quality product due to fish being damaged by difficulty in handling the fish on wire nets used to support them over the fire;
o loss of smoke and heat, resulting in uneven smoking;

o limited capacity of smoking larger volumes of fish;
o time-consuming in terms of the amount of time needed to handle the fish during smoking.

## Socio-economic background

Nyanyano is a fishing community twenty-two miles from Accra, where twenty women smoke fish using the 'Chorkor smoker'. Eighty per cent of these women are married but live apart from their husbands.

Participation in polygamous relationships is both socially acceptable and an economic necessity for a woman. It is only through marriage with a man who owns a boat that she can be assured of regular supplies of fish to smoke. In return, the wives are responsible for taking turns feeding the husband with part of the funds made from her sales. In this sense, sharing the financial burden with other wives becomes attractive.

Fish smoking is traditionally done on an individual or family basis, composed of three to four family members which may include a mother and daughters or group of sisters. Sometimes individuals will break off from these groups once they have acquired the working capital to set up business on their own.

Lack of capital and access to low interest loans is a major constraint to purchasing more fish and thereby taking advantage of the increased smoking capacity of the Chorkor technology.

The fish is purchased from fishermen (their husbands) who demand immediate cash payment for the day's catch which has been allocated to each wife. Lack of cash to purchase increasing amounts of fish also becomes compounded when there is a shortage of petrol, forcing fuel prices up. Given these constraints, it has been difficult for Nyanyano women to realize the full benefit of the improved oven in order to substantially increase their income.

The system of obtaining bank loans has also created a structural constraint for women fish smokers, in that commercial banks prefer lending to groups, although this is not how the women customarily organize themselves for this activity.

The National Council for Women had previously assisted the women in forming fish smoking groups in 1984 by commissioning the initial construction of fifteen improved Chorkor ovens. This group subsequently met once a week in order to discuss matters such as acquiring further smokers, and various problems encountered including access to credit, fish storage and marketing. Individual contributions were made with the goal of seeking a group loan from the bank. Possibly the concept of group formation was not fully accepted by each member, as meetings became irregular when project staff attendance at their meetings declined. The initial goal was never realized and the group disbanded.

## Advantages and disadvantages of the technology

The Chorkor smoker has been accepted by individual women who have constructed these ovens with their own funds. Women who previously did not smoke fish have taken on this activity having had improved smokers constructed for them. Changes in old processing methods have occurred as a result of the introduction of the Chorkor oven. Fish was previously dried in the sand due to lack of capacity in their traditional ovens; but using Chorkor ovens they are now able to smoke all their fish. Traditional cylindrical mud ovens have assumed a new purpose: storing the smoked fish. It is believed that these traditional ovens would be abandoned completely if improved storage technologies were available.

The new technology has assisted women in relieving them of the most laborious process of arranging the fish in alternate layers using sticks and broomsticks, as required with the mud ovens. Trays within the improved ovens have replaced this step thus making the process more efficient and reducing damage done to the fish, which tends to lower the value, in handling. Two smoking ovens were required in the old method of turning whereas one improved oven is sufficient for turning.

The Chorkor oven has also had an effect on marketing possibilities. Fish that is smoked with the improved oven is usually bought first and can demand higher prices. As they have been producing under capacity, for reasons mentioned earlier, fish processors 'mammies' have not been able to take full advantage of this potential to increase income.

Time inputs were examined, comparing time spent on fish smoking with the traditional and improved ovens. In the peak season, women can smoke as many as ten crates of fish (600kg) taking the whole day to arrange the fish from one traditional cylindrical oven to the next. Not enough time was available during this period to cook for their children who were instead given money to buy cooked food. The improved smoker required less time for smoking. It could smoke fifteen crates of fish a day whereas the cylindrical oven could only take six crates per day. In addition, the tray system saves further time as arranging fish using the old method took more time than stacking trays.

The women felt that the ten trays introduced in one smoking cycle could be increased in order to avoid wasting firewood and increase the smoking capacity of the oven further.

Problems mentioned were that the improved smoker could not be operated by one person; the cross-piece of wood dividing the tray into two can catch fire if the flames grow too high, and smoking smaller quantities of fish wastes fuel as the design of the oven does not compartmentalize the areas holding the firewood.

Some of the ovens subsequently introduced into Nyanyano were a modification of the original Chorkor oven (even though they are referred to as Chorkor ovens). The modification included removal of the original middle wall and insertion of two pieces of iron rod fixed to the upper middle part of the oven on which the trays are rested. This caused problems with trays catching fire, and by making the capacity too large. In the original design the middle wall was put in to prevent the trays catching fire and to be able to smoke smaller quantities of fish by using only half of the oven.

Reliance on informal money lenders presented a higher risk to women as interest rates from them were high. As mentioned earlier, formal commercial banks were not accommodating to individual loan applications. Lack of available capital was seen as a major constraint in increasing output and for women who did not participate in the initial group scheme to purchase the new technology. Money relationships between husband (fisherman) and wife (fish processor) place further financial constraints upon the woman as spot-payment is demanded, not giving any period in which to take advantage of storage methods allowing her to demand higher prices during lean seasons.

The price of fish is expressed as a standard quantity determined by the base price established each day when the first boat returns from its fishing trip. This set price is often, not surprisingly, open to debate between men and women.

Internal family relationships can also play a positive role in the organization of fish processing. Mothers will usually co-operate with married and unmarried daughters as a team until a daughter has the financial means to form a separate unit. As head of a team, the mother has full control over the fish, providing initial cash payment for the fish, organizing the marketing, retaining the profits and finally providing money for cooking meals.

(ILO, 1985)

# Chorkor oven – Guinea and Togo

The Republic of Guinea, with its very long (300km) coastline is capable of supporting a mixed fishing industry. Artisanal fishing accounts for about 26 000 tonnes per year, of which a large part is processed by smoking, primarily carried out by women. However, because the methods used are traditional, they are labour-intensive, and both fuel- and time-consuming.

In answer to requests from the Republic of Guinea, in 1984 UNIFEM provided funds for a project introducing an improved fish smoking technology. The immediate objectives of the project included regrouping three hundred women into co-operatives for the processing and distribution of fish, and introducing an improved fish smoking kiln to reduce women's labour, improve working conditions, and increase productivity and revenue. The project was to construct the smoking ovens in the capital, as well as in two villages in the interior of the country, at Boffa, to exploit lake fisheries.

The improved smoking technology introduced was the Chorkor oven originating in Ghana, where it had been widely tested and used. The Chorkor is a rectangular clay brick oven with two openings at the front of the fire. The fish is placed on trays (made of chicken wire) which are stacked on top of the oven. Up to fifteen trays can be stacked on the oven with a total of between 100kg to 160kg of fish being smoked at a time.

As part of the project eight project personnel, including a carpenter and mason, were sent to Ghana and Benin to familiarize themselves with the Chorkor and be trained in its construction, use and maintenance.

## Advantages and disadvantages of the project

It was found that after two years the project had obtained certain positive results despite the numerous difficulties it faced. Some of the setbacks included a change in the political situation of the country which resulted in changes in the economy, notably increases in the cost of living; and materials for the construction of trays were not available in Guinea.

Most of the original members of the co-operative were not traditional fish-smokers. They therefore regarded participation in the project more in terms of salaried employment rather than independent use of commonly owned facilities. This emphasizes the need for careful definition of criteria for the selection of beneficiaries before a project commences.

The women did not have a regular supply of fish to smoke; in some cases women would pay for transport to come to the centre, but had not been able to smoke fish. The fishermen, who prior to the political changes had agreed to supply the centre with fresh fish, then refused to provide it or would do so only at exorbitant prices which the women could not afford. Consequently the women have resorted to smoking frozen fish. This means that not only is the fish processed twice, but energy is wasted as well.

Although the Chorkor can smoke up to fifteen trays of fish, it was noted that in most cases women used only up to five trays at a time because there is not a sufficient supply of fish to warrant the use of more trays. In the interior of the country where fish is obtained from lakes, the problem of availability of fish is dependent on social factors. In some cases the fishermen sell the catch to any women who are able to buy, even if the women are not their wives. These women then sometimes market the fish fresh. In other instances the fishermen may sell only to their wives; thus women entering into a fish smoking co-operative are at a disadvantage if their husbands are not fishermen. In a few cases in Guinea, women supply the fishermen with enough petrol to pay for one fishing trip; in return they are obliged to supply the women with the entire catch.

Additionally, there is increased competition between the fishermen with motorized boats and those with non-motorized boats. The latter are unable to get a sufficient catch each time as they can only travel to catch fish at limited distances, whereas fishermen with motorized boats can provide fish but have to take into account the cost of the motor and fuel, thus increasing the price of fish.

In terms of the technical advantages and disadvantages of the Chorkor it is clear that in the Guinean context, the Chorkor is an improved technology. Traditional smoking systems consisted of 'open smokers' which were basically a grill on four wooden legs — fuel consumption is considerably higher in these traditional ovens. The Chorkor presents a marked improvement in that it is a 'closed system' — the fire is enclosed in a compartment, in the bottom of the rectangular oven so fuel consumption is much less. The trays, however, become heavy once the fish are placed on them and require two women to manipulate one tray. When more than seven trays are stacked they are very difficult to manage in terms of weight and height. As a result, some women are reverting to their traditional ovens but covering the sides with sheets of metal, corrugated iron or similar material to enclose the fire and thus reduce the amount of wood consumed.

Currently the project staff are working with the women to adapt the Chorkor to address these needs.

From the points mentioned above, it is clear that not only is the technology itself important when assessing its relevance, but also the situation into which it is introduced. If the social, economic and political conditions in a village do not allow the women access to a regular supply of fish, then the expense of an oven with greater productivity is not worthwhile. However, if the oven will reduce the amount of fuel needed, so reducing costs within an existing productive system, then the savings need to be examined. This saving should also be assessed in terms of women's labour and time. One reason for using the Chorkor is to reduce women's labour constraints. However, problems in lifting and carrying the trays prevented this aim from being realized. While there are still problems with the Chorkor in Guinea, it has proved to be a significant improvement in terms of fuel consumption.

## Replication in Togo

In Togo, the Chorkor was introduced in order to increase productivity and revenue and reduce the amount of fuel and labour required. The scale of the project in Togo was much smaller than in Guinea, although the impact was significant. The project initially constructed twelve Chorkor smokers at various villages along the coast. Since then between fifty and eighty additional Chorkor smokers have been built by women individually.

This is an indication that the advantages of the Chorkor have been realized. However, like the Guinean women, Togolese women are also suffering from an insufficient supply of fish. This is largely due to the fact that there are no strong fishing traditions in Togo. Consequently, the women have to rely on foreign fishermen, usually Ghanaians, and therefore the supply of fish is irregular, leaving the women unable to count on a regular income. Women whose husbands are fishermen do have better access to fish, especially if their husbands run motorized boats. There is a tradition of the fishermen selling the catch to their wives.

The replication of the Chorkor smoker is a positive result of the project. However, there is a problem with proper replication of the smokers. Where artisans (carpenters, masons) were trained to build the smokers, no problems were experienced, but in cases where the women themselves were building the smokers or hiring untrained artisans, there have been problems with the dimensions of the trays, fire holes and smokers. This has resulted in trays being burned or of increased fuel consumption. Thus, although there has been some positive replication, there is a need to monitor the spread of the Chorkors to ensure that they are correctly built and properly used.
(Harmandip Sandhu, UNIFEM)

## Altona ovens – Sierra Leone

Tombo village is in the western area of Sierra Leone with strong historical, structural and economic links with Freetown, the capital. Fishing and fish processing are the main economic activities and the main sources of employment for 90 per cent of Tombo's population. Tombo village experienced rapid socio-economic changes starting in the 1950s when Mfantse fishermen from Ghana came to Sierra Leone bringing their fishing and fish processing expertise which changed the local economy from small-scale subsistence fishing to a more cash-orientated system. A large number of migrants were attracted, and profits increased. As the volume of fish for processing grew, requiring more labour, innovations in technology were sought.

The Ghanaians introduced the present banda (traditional smoking oven) design of mud and bricks supported by iron or wooden poles and covered with a wire-mesh grill layer. Some households even constructed multiple bandas to meet increasing processing demands. Sun-drying, combined with salting, was used for tiny fish.

This increase in fish production resulted in the creation of new long-distance markets throughout Sierra Leone. Women fish traders from the capital travelled to Tombo to buy fish in wholesale quantities. Professional women could market the fish as far as Liberia and Guinea.

## Women processors within the household

Seventy-five per cent of Tombo women are directly involved in fish processing and marketing activities. Most women have buying arrangements with boat owners, with each woman buying from only one boat owner (usually her husband) but sometimes buying from others by special arrangement.

From this point on, women make the decisions to act independently from men and keep separate budgets. Processing activities are organized by the first wife who owns the banda, buys the fresh fish and sells the smoked fish. The junior wives are involved in washing the fish, transporting them from the beach to banda, watching the fire, and other tasks designated by the first wife.

Processing is very labour-intensive. The women spend twelve hours of continuous work processing 600 dozen herring (400kg) using a typical banda with a capacity of 100–1200 dozen herring. During the dry season, most women will spend up to seventy-five hours a week on processing.

Women control the marketing of foodstuffs such as smoked fish. A complex system of long distance trade involving wholesalers, semi-wholesalers, traders, and retailers has developed.

The changing socio-economic structure has affected the women's position within the household. Husbands and senior wives operate as a team in this whole cycle, but still keep separate accounts. Women invest in their husband's fishing operations, providing loans in order to expand fishing activities by purchase of boats, engines, nets etc.

The money earned by women from the sale of processed and marketed fish is the major cash source for the household. The income from their economic activities has provided a cushion for men when fishing has become difficult due to climatic or other reasons.

## Tombo village fisheries pilot project

The pilot project was jointly sponsored by the governments of Sierra Leone and the Federal Republic of Germany and initiated in 1981 to last for five years. It was a pilot project to be replicated in other fishing villages on the western coast of Africa. Under the sponsorship of GTZ, the operating budget was quite substantial (US$ 6.5 million). The philosophy of the project was that improvements in fishing techniques should go hand in hand with innovations in processing techniques and marketing strategies, the latter being the special economic domain of women in African fishing communities.

The aim of promoting changes in fishing technologies was to reduce the high operating costs for fishermen via improvements in fishing gear, boat-building, introduction of sails and fuel-saving diesel engines. Any increase in the catch would of course affect the women processors in terms of workload.

Improvements in fish processing concerned themselves with the introduction of the Ghanaian model of the Altona-type oven. The project staff in consultation with women modified the design by lowering the height, expanding the width and using trays made of iron. Although these changes increased the price, the ovens were easier and safer to operate. Savings in fuel costs of 60 per cent, a lifespan of almost double that of the traditional banda, decreased processing time (including laying) and the fact that constant supervision of the fish over the fire was no longer required, were seen as improvements.

Disadvantages were also observed: handling the trays required two people, and frequent changes in the position of the trays in order to accommodate the temperature gradients within the oven were extra work for the junior wives. Handling the hot, fully loaded trays could cause accidents such as burns to the stomach. The technology was inappropriate within the context of the deteriorating economic conditions in the country. The materials needed to build and maintain the oven such as iron, steel and firebricks (locally made mud bricks could not withstand the high temperatures) proved too costly to replicate after the original dozen were built. In addition, no locally trained

mason was capable of building these ovens.

The Altona oven was seen as useful if there was a small batch of fish to cure, but was generally not capable of handling the large volume of fish available to processors in this area.

The three-plus years generally needed to pay for the oven was seen as too long a payback period in light of the low material investment needed for more traditional ovens. The women processors were purchasing such high volumes of fish to process that the savings in fuelwood costs were seen as negligible in terms of the investment cost of the Altona oven.

Fish processing arrangements in Tombo are part of a socially defined hierarchy of multiple wives. The construction of the Altona oven upset this hierarchy. The trays were very heavy, with the highest of the two dozen trays to be shifted being two metres from the ground. Two women could not shift these trays, and only men were strong enough to do this work.

The Altona oven programme ceased and no further ovens were built from 1982 to 1986. The original twelve individuals who were given the ovens reneged on the project loan and there was no one in an extension role to follow up the case and seek payment. However, the twelve processors have fully accepted the Altona oven and no longer use the traditional ovens.

There have been technology adaptations in Tombo resulting in the traditional banda almost disappearing and continuing increases in the production of the Fante banda. The Fante banda is basically a modified traditional oven with built-up sides and increased surface area (up to twelve metres square) to support the higher volume of fish requiring processing. As the capability to catch fish has increased, so has the size of the banda.

In general, the upkeep of these bandas is poor, because of lack of materials such as metal for the grates and concrete to reinforce the mud blocks. It was under discussion that the project would purchase these materials from outside with foreign exchange and set up a store for fish mammies much the same as it has done with making fishing gear available to the fishermen.

The project was extended for two years. The initial goal of increasing the volume of protein available in Sierra Leone by large-scale introduction of fish gear and processing technologies was altered in order to focus on increasing overall community development. No more new technologies will be introduced, in recognition of the multiple economic and social problems that emerged with previous technologies. A sociologist was appointed and the aim of project activities is to expand both women's and community group links to the project. (Steady, F.C.; Kotnik, A., 1982)

# 5
# Planning a project or enterprise

FROM THE SELECTION of case studies presented in Chapter 4, some questions emerge which should be asked by project planners and decision makers before they proceed with the implementation of a fish processing project or promotion of a fish processing enterprise.

Some questions, particularly socio-economic issues, are of fundamental importance and must be addressed in baseline data or feasibility studies at the initial stages of project planning. Looking at the questions below may draw attention to areas where more information is needed before project implementation can go ahead. Other questions, particularly those concerned purely with technical information, may be answered (having carried out the initial studies) with simple one- or two-sentence or yes/no answers.

The first questions are concerned with the viability of the enterprise; then there are questions about the role of women in traditional processing, with subsidiary questions listed below the main question where appropriate; and finally the impact of improved technologies is considered.

---

## First questions

---

1. Why set up a small-scale fish processing venture?
   o Is there a market for increased yields?
   o Can the existing system cope with increased demand?
   o If yes to the above, how will you improve/add capacity?
2. When processing a given quantity of fish using the traditional process, what inputs are required?
   o How much time is required?
   o What is the labour input required from males and females for each activity or stage?
   o How much fuel is used, and is it readily available?
   o What quantity of fish is yielded?
   o What is the value of the inputs (raw materials, fuel, water, packaging) in comparison with the output?

---

## Background questions

---

1. What exactly is the place of women in traditional processing? What role do they play in the different stages?
   o What is the traditional marketing mechanism and who controls it? (Do women have access to markets?)

- o What proportion of the income from the processed fish do women earn and keep?
- o What are the major problems and difficulties of women producers in this field?
2. What is the extent of traditional and small-scale fish processing in the area?
   - o What is the traditional process?
   - o Are there different traditional methods of processing the fish?   Yes ☐   No ☐
   - o Which method tends to be used most frequently, and why?
   - o Does the main method vary in different parts of the country?
   (It is important to know about the various traditional methods being used, as this may influence the improvements needed.)
3. Who owns the raw material?
   - o Are there more fish available than can be processed in the traditional manner?                                                                Y ☐        N ☐
   - o Are there ever seasonal shortages of fresh fish? When?          Y ☐        N ☐
   - o What is done with the by-products of processing?

---

# Effects of improved technology on traditional processing industry

## Technical considerations

1. Will the use of the improved technology reduce labour input as compared with the traditional method? How?
2. What is the capacity of the improved technology — will it be able to cope with the demands of processing in terms of quantity of fish available to processors?
3. Will the equipment produce a greater quantity of and better quality processed fish than traditional means? (Will the fish have a different taste — if so, will it be acceptable?)
4. What will be the processing rate of the fish?
5. Will the process be faster?                                            Y ☐        N ☐
6. What are the water/fuel/power requirements of the equipment?
7. Will the users be able to meet those requirements?                     Y ☐        N ☐
8. Will use of the equipment require a change in packaging Y ☐   N ☐ or transport of the fish? Y ☐     N ☐
9. Are there ways of producing equipment and/or spares locally           Y ☐        N ☐
10. Can the equipment be maintained using local resources?
    - o are spare parts available?                                        Y ☐        N ☐
    - o can local artisans repair the machinery Y ☐    N ☐, or do they need to be trained? Y ☐     N ☐
11. Will the users be able to afford the added cost of spare parts?       Y ☐        N ☐
12. Will the users of the equipment need to be trained?
    - o will they need technical training Y ☐    N ☐ and if so, how much?
    - o is training locally available?                                    Y ☐        N ☐
    - o is there already some familiarity with this type of technology?   Y ☐        N ☐

## Socio-economic considerations

1. What is the cost of the machine and related equipment?
2. Is the cost manageable on an individual or community basis?
3. If credit is needed, is it accessible? Will the women be able to repay the loan?
4. What will the return on the investment be? What will the monthly profit be?
5. How many years will it take the operator to cover the cost of the machine?
6. Who will control use of the machine? Will it be co-operatively controlled or will individual men or women manage it?
7. Who will earn the income after processing?
8. Would availability of the improved technology increase women's income generation?
   - if not, why not?
   - what proportion of the income would women earn?
   - would fish processing remain a significant income-generating activity for women after introduction of the equipment?
9. Will introduction of the equipment bring about any change in the pattern of work and work habits? How?
   - male
   - female
10. Will there be a change in the daily schedule required to do any task?
11. Does the improved equipment require more or less fresh fish than traditional methods?
12. If it requires more, is that supply available and who owns it?
13. Will the improved method change the traditional market mechanisms?
14. If more fish is processed can the market cope with the increase and will this affect the price?
15. What will happen to the by-products (if any) from the improved method?
16. If by-products are sold, who will earn the income?
17. Will the users be able to cope with the consequential requirements of effective enterprise development such as handling employees, market and price negotiations, and cash flow?

# Illustrated guide

## Kench salting (Dry pile)

The fish are layered flesh to flesh, skin to skin, and the top layer of fish are skin side upwards. Weights can be used to press the pile. The brine formed is allowed to drain away.

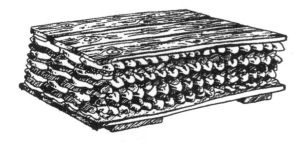

## Pickle curing (Wet pile)

The fish and salt are layered (as for kench salting) inside a container (for example a margarine tin), which is then sealed carefully, labelled and left to cure.

**Traditional smoking pit in East Africa**

**Traditional Ghanaian cylindrical mud oven**

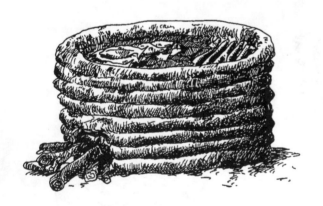

*a) Open*

*b) With thatched cover*

## Traditional smoking platforms or 'bandas' in Sierra Leone

The metal sheeting (often made from a flattened oil drum) covering the open sides of the banda helps to conserve fuel.

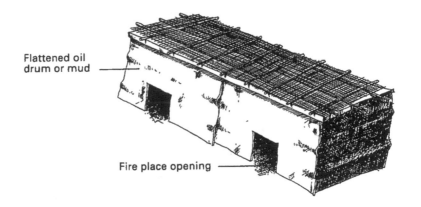

Flattened oil drum or mud

Fire place opening

*a) Enclosed*

*b) Open*

## Evaporative coolers

The fish is hung or placed on trays inside the open weave container which is stood on a raised platform in water. A wet cloth covers the fish and hangs over the water so that it is continuously re-wetted. The action of water evaporating from the cloth cools the fish.

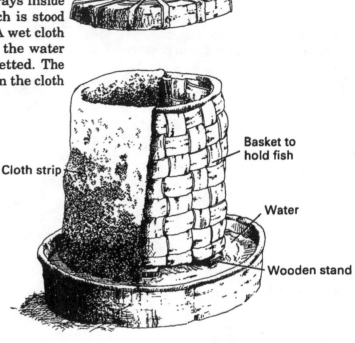

Basket to hold fish

Cloth strip

Water

Wooden stand

The evaporative charcoal cooler works on the same principle. In this design the water filters down from the top of the cooler. It passes over the charcoal, which is encased in wire mesh, from which the water evaporates to cool the interior of the box.

Cloth strip

Wooden frame for water tray

Charcoal covered in wire mesh

## Drying rack

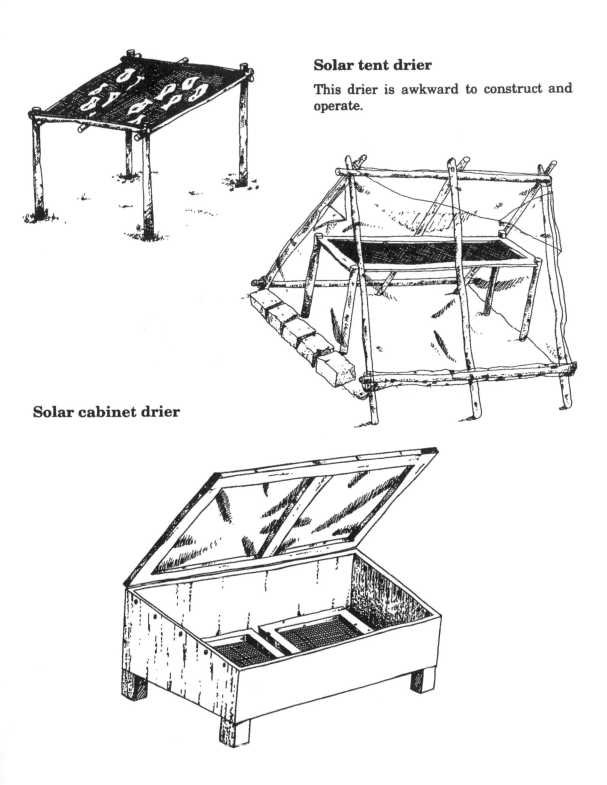

## Solar tent drier

This drier is awkward to construct and operate.

## Solar cabinet drier

## Solar dome drier

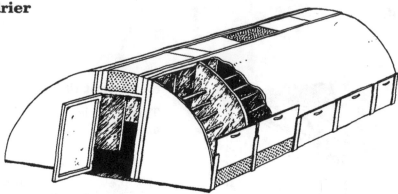

## Solar drier with separate collector and drying chamber

The chimney is painted black to absorb more heat. This will help to heat the air inside the chimney, thereby increasing the air flow through the drier.

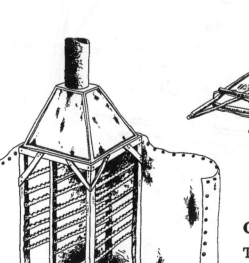

## Canvas drier

This is a direct convection drier constructed from a wooden frame covered by a canvas awning which encloses the drying chamber. The roof and chimney are made from galvanized iron. The drier is fuelled by charcoal in a fire box or cement pit below the drying chamber.

## Tray drier

When rain threatens, the trays previously placed to sun-dry the fish are assembled on top of each other over a simple heating compartment. A roof and chimney are placed on top and drying continues by direct heating using charcoal.

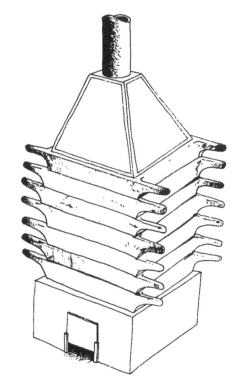

## IRRI Vortex fish drier

The Vortex wind machine is placed on top of the drying chamber and rotates in the wind. This causes a draught of air through the drying chamber.

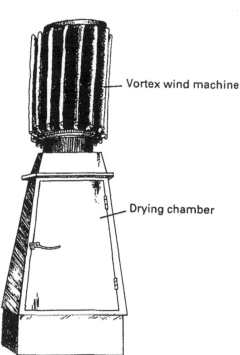

Vortex wind machine

Drying chamber

## Low-cost fish drier

This is a vertical tray drier fuelled by coconut husks, firewood or rice husks. At
the base of the fire is a combustion chamber made of concrete. Attached to one side
is the incinerator made of asbestos and
metal into which the fuel is placed.

A heat exchanger is housed across the
incinerator and combustion chamber and
heated air passes into the drying chamber. Wooden framed wire mesh trays are
positioned centrally within the drying
chamber. At the bottom of the concrete
chamber there are ten air vents with slid-
ing covers. A chimney with an inverted,
L-shaped hood placed on top of the drying
chamber increases air flow within the
drier.

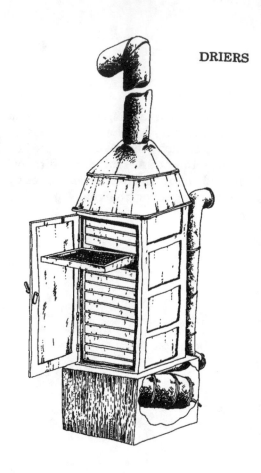

## UPLB-IDRC drier

This drier is composed of four principal
parts: a brick furnace, the heat exchanger, the blower and the drying chamber. It is fired by rice husks and an
average of 25kg of fuel per hour are consumed. Air is heated by the heat exchanger and is sucked by the blower into
the drying chamber where the air temperature is in the range of 40–60°C. The
drying chamber has five compartments
and a uniform temperature distribution is
achieved by adjusting the exhaust vents
on top of each compartment.

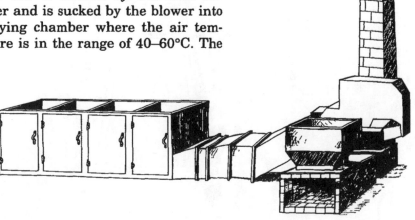

## Solar agro-waste multipurpose drier/smoker

The SAM-type drier is a rectangular box made of metal with a tapering roof. The drying chamber holds twelve pairs of trays. The roof, the door and the side facing it are made of polythene sheeting. The chimney attached to the roof is made of metal and air flow through the chamber is regulated by a damper. A furnace is situated below the drying chamber and is separated by a piece of corrugated sheet metal.

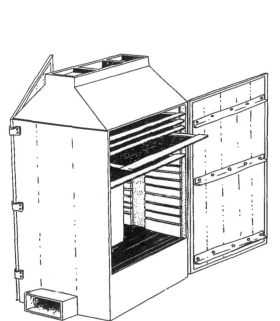

## Steel drier

This drier is constructed entirely of steel and comprises a firebox and flue which passes through the centre of the drying chamber. The furnace is fired by coconut husks, firewood or charcoal. Fish are placed on wire trays positioned either side of the central chimney.

## Mud and pole smoking kiln

Designed as a development of the oil
drum smoker, the mud and pole kiln is
constructed from locally available materials such as bamboo sticks, leaves and
mud. There is separate fire box delivering
heat into the smoking chamber via an underground flue or smoke pipe. (Clucas, I.)

## Oil drum smoker

Cylindrical ovens made by joining two
opened oil drums are used by artisanal
processors. A stoke hole is cut at the base
of the oven in which a fire is made. A per-
forated metal sheet can be inserted inside
the drum just above the fire to act as a
smoke spreader. Trays are suspended to-
wards the top of the drum to hold the fish.

## Watanabe drum smoker

This smoker is constructed from an
oil drum, much like the one in the
preceding figure, except that there
is a separate enclosed fire box and
connecting pipe for better control
over the smoking process.

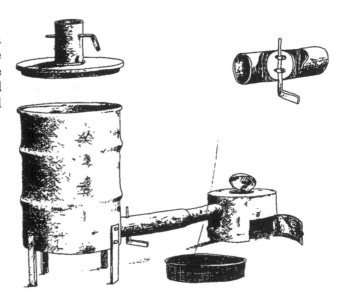

## Altona-type oven

The simple version of an Altona oven consists of a brick or cement fire box located
below a smoking chamber made of metal.
The fish are placed on trays which slide
into the smoking chamber. Many other
versions of this kiln have been constructed using less expensive materials
such as mud or fired bricks instead of
metal. A more complex design built of cement known as the Rogers kiln, was introduced to Uganda. However, with both
the Altona-type and the Rogers kilns, the
initial cost of construction makes them
unaffordable for artisans. Although the
Rogers kiln was still being used in
Uganda some time after its introduction,
the fish processors had not built any
others themselves.

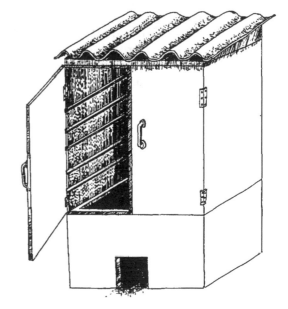

## Adjetey oven

The Adjetey oven was designed in Ghana to overcome the two main problems of the traditional cylindrical oven: an increased holding capacity for fish and greater control over the fire. The oven is made of iron and consists of a stand, a smoking chamber and a fire box. The oven is fired indirectly and a metal tube connects the fire box to the smoking chamber. The oven is rectangular with an inverted conical top providing a vent at the top, equipped with a simple damper to regulate air flow.

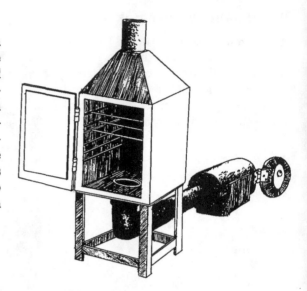

## Ivory Coast kiln

First introduced to the Ivory Coast, this smoker can be made easily from locally-available materials. The trays of fish are stacked on top of a base made from sheet metal (flattened oil drum) or asbestos roofing sheet. A fire box and a smoke spreader are enclosed in the base.

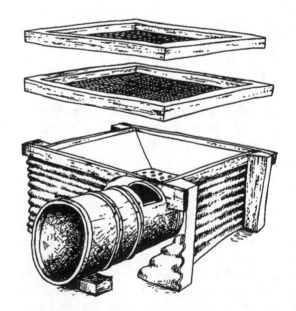

## Chorkor smoker

Originally designed in Ghana to resemble the traditional rectangular smoking kilns, the Chorkor smoker contains two stoke holes along one of its sides. Wooden trays fitted with wire mesh are stacked on top of the rectangular base and can be alternated during smoking.

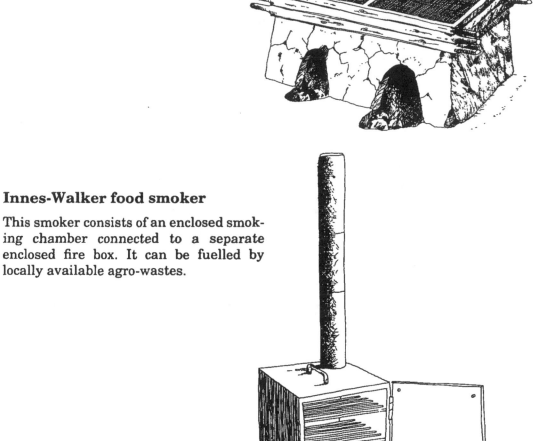

## Innes-Walker food smoker

This smoker consists of an enclosed smoking chamber connected to a separate enclosed fire box. It can be fuelled by locally available agro-wastes.

# References

Adams, M.R., Cooke, R.D. and Pongpen Rattagool (1985)
'Fermented Fish Products of South East Asia.' *Tropical Science* 25, pp. 61–75.

Beck, U. and During, S.E. (1986)
'Development Aspects of Village Based Fish Processing Methods in Sierra Leone, West Africa. An Appraisal of some Technical, Social, Environmental and Economic Factors.' In *Cured Fish Production in the Tropics*. Reilly, A. and Barile, L.E., (eds.) pp. 186–223.

Bostock et al. (1985)
'The use of solar dryers in the production of high quality salted and dried fish; guide for producers and profile of economic feasibility.' *Boletín Científico y Técnico*, Vol. III, No. 10, Instituto de Pesca, Casilla 5918, Guayaquil, Ecuador (English & Spanish).

Bostock, T.W., Coulter, J.P., Camba, N., Mora, Y. (1986)
'The production and marketing of salted small pelagic fish for rural consumption.' *Boletín Científico y Técnico*. Vol. VIII, No. 8, Instituto Nacional de Pesca, Casilla 5918, Guayaqil, Ecuador (Spanish).

Brenndorfer, B., Kennedy, L., Oswin Batelman, C.O., Trim, D.S., Mrema, G.C., Wereko-Brobby, C. (1985)
*Solar Dryers – Their Role in Post-Harvest Processing*. Commonwealth Science Council Commonwealth Secretariat Publications, London.

Brownell, W. (1983)
*A Practical Guide to Improved Fish Smoking in West Africa – Introducing the Chorkor Smoker*. NCWD/FRI. UNICEF, New York.

Bulaong, S., Reilly, A.M., Orejana, F.M. (1986)
'Study of the Mycoflora of Smoked Roundscad (Decapterus Macrosoma Bleeker) from Malabon – Tondo Areas.' In *Cured Fish Production in the Tropics*. Reilly, A. and Barile, L.E., (eds.) pp. 162–173.

Clucas, I.J. (1982)
*Fish Handling, Preservation and Processing in the Tropics: Part 2*. Report of the Tropical Development and Research Institute, G145, VIII, p. 144.

Curran, C.A., N'jai, A.E., Nequaye-Tetteh, G., Diouf, N. (1985)
*Testing a Solar Dome Fish Dryer in The Gambia*. FAO Fish Rep. (329) Suppl. pp. 173–184.

Duere, J.D. and Dryer, W.J. (1952)
*J. Fish Res. Bd.* Canada 8, pp. 325–331.

ECA, Addis Ababa (1984)
*Women in the Artisanal Fishing Industry in Senegal and Ghana*. African Training and Research Centre for Women E/ECA/ATRCW/84/04.

FAO/DANIDA (undated)
*Fish Preservation 1. Salting*. Speaker's commentary for filmstrip series on fish-handling practices.

FAO/DANIDA (undated)
*Fish Preservation II. Smoking-Drying*. Speaker's commentary for filmstrip series on fish-handling practices.

FAO/DANIDA (undated)
*Fish Preservation III. Drying.* Speaker's commentary for filmstrip series on fish-handling practices.

FAO/DANIDA (undated)
*How Perla Improved Her Fish Stall and How Business Improved.* Speaker's commentary for the filmstrip series on fish-handling practices.

FAO (1970)
*Smoke Curing of Fish.* FAO Fish Report (88): 43p.

FAO (1981)
*The prevention of losses in cured fish.* FAO Fish Technical Paper, (219): 87p.

ILO/Government of Norway (1984)
*Improved Village Technology for Women's Activities – a Manual for West Africa.*

ILO (1985)
*Field Report on Post-Adoption Studies Technologies for Rural Women. ILO / NETH / 80 / GHA (1).*

ILO/FAO (1982)
*Small-scale processing of fish.* Technology Series. Technical Memorandum, No. 3.

Jeon, Y.W., Halos, L.S., Belonio, A., Elepaño, A. (1986)
'The IRRI Warehouse Drying System.' In *Fish Production in the Tropics.* Reilly, A. and Barile, L.E. (eds.) pp. 91–107.

Kotnik, A. (1982)
*Women in Small-scale Fisheries. The Case of Tombo Village / Sierra Leone.* Contribution of the Republic of Sierra Leone and the Federal Republic of Germany. Promotion of Small-Scale Fisheries. No. 2, 1982 (Sierra Leone/GTZ).

Lupin, H.M. (1985)
*How to Determine the Right Fish-to-Ice Ratio for Insulated Fish Containers.* FAO Fish Report (329). Supplement.

Nerquaye-Tetteh, G., Eyeson, K.K., Tete-Marmon, J. (1978)
'Studies on "Bomone" – A Ghanaian Fermented Fish Product.' (Accepted for publication in Ghana Journal of Agricultural Science).

Orejana, F.M. and Embuscado, M.E. (1983)
*A New Solar-Agrowaste Smoker-Drier for Fish and Shellfish.* FAO Fish Report (279) Supplement pp. 133–146.

Parry, R.W.H. (1986)
'Brining and Pressing of Small Pelagic Fish as an Alternative to Traditional Processing.' In *Cured Fish Production in the Tropics.* Reilly, A. and Barile, L.E., (eds.), pp. 84–90.

Reaño, J.R. (1986)
'Processing and Marketing of Cured Fish in Peru.' In *Cured Fish Production in the Tropics.* Reilly, A. and Barile, L.E., (eds.) pp. 73–78.

Roberts, S.F. (1986)
'Methods of Fish Salting.' In *Cured Fish Production in the Tropics.* Reilly, A. and Barile, L.E. (eds.) pp. 56–62.

Roberts, S.F. (1986)
'Agrowaste Fish Dryers.' In *Cured Fish Production in the Tropics.* Reilly, A. and Barile, L.E. (eds.) pp. 108–130.

Sison, E.C., Garcia, V.V., Carpio, E.V., Alcantara, Jr., P.R., Madamba, C.S.P. (1983)
*Adaption of Artificial Fish Drying Technology in the Philippines.* FAO Fish Report, (279) Supplement pp. 109–122.

66                                                     REFERENCES/FURTHER READING

Steady, F.C. (undated)
*Women's Work in Rural Cash Food Systems: The Tombo Development Project, Sierra Leone.*

Stroud, G.D. (1986)
*A Technical and Economic Appraisal of Artisanal Smoking Ovens in Ghana.* Field Document FAO Fisheries Department. TCP/GHA/4506 (T).

Trim, D.S. and Curran, C.A. (1983)
*A Comparative Study of Solar and Sun-Drying of Fish in Ecuador.* Report of the Tropical Development and Research Institute. L60, VI, 44p.

Villadsen, A. and Flores, F. (1983)
*Low-cost, Agro-Waste Fish Drier Development.* FAO Fish Report, (279) Supplement pp. 123–132.

# Further reading

Bostock, T.W., Walker, D.J. and Wood, C.D. (1987)
*Reduction of Losses in Cured Fish in the Tropics — Guide for Extension Workers.* Report of the Tropical Development and Research Institute, G204, V. 47p.

Clucas, I.J. (1981)
*Fish Handling, Preservation and Processing in the Tropics: part 1.* Report of the Tropical Development and Research Institute, G144, VIII, 144p.

Drewes, E. (1986)
*Activating Fisherwomen for Development through Trained Link Workers in Tamil Nadu, India.* Development of small-scale fisheries in the Bay of Bengal, Madras, FAO/SIDA. BOBP/REP/27, 44p.

FAO (1980)
*International Directory of Fish Technology Institutes.* Fish Utilisation and Marketing Service, Fishery Industries Division, Fisheries Department. FAO Fish Technical Paper, (152) Ref. 1, 106p.

FAO (1982)
Proceedings of the FAO Expert Consultation on Fish Technology in Africa, Casablanca, Morocco, 7–11 June 1982. FAO Fish Report (268) Supplement 288p.

FAO (1986)
*Fish Processing in Africa.* Proceedings of the FAO Expert Consultation on Fish Technology in Africa, Lusaka, Zambia, 21–25 January 1985. FAO Fish Report (329) Supplement 474p.

ILO (1985)
*Fish Smoking Technologies for Rural Women – Ghana.* Technical Manual No. 3 ILO, Geneva.

James, D. (ed.) (1983)
*The Production and Storage of Dried Fish.* Proceedings of the workshop on the production and storage of dried fish. University Pertanian Malaysia, Serdang (Malaysia), 2–5 November 1982. FAO Fish Report (279) Supplement, 265p.

Mackie, I.M., Hardy, R. and Hobbs, G. (1971)
*Fermented Fish Products.* FAO Fish Report (100), 54p.

Pollnac, R.B. (1985)
*'Social and Cultural Characteristics in Small-Scale Fishery Development.'* In *Putting People First.* Cernea, M.M. (ed.). World Bank pp. 187–223.

Randall, P.E. (undated)
*Women in Fish Production*, FAO Regional Office for Africa for UN–Decade for Women–Equality–Development–Peace.

Reilly, A. and Barile, L.E. (eds.) (1986)
*Cured Fish Production in the Tropics.* Proceedings of a Workshop on the Production of Cured Fish, University of the Philippines in the Visayas, 14–25 April, 1986.

Rogers, J.F. (1970)
*Improved Cement Block Fish Smoking Kiln.* Uganda Occasional Papers, No.3.

Rogers, J.F., Cole, R.C. and Smith, J.D. (1975)
*An Illustrated Guide to Fish Preparation.* Report of the Tropical Development and Research Institute, G83, 73p.

Tropical Products Institute (1977)
Proceedings of the Conference on the Handling, Processing and Marketing of Tropical Fish, 5–9 July, 1976.

# Contacts

## Africa

**FRI**
Food Research Institute, PO Box M20, Accra, Ghana.

**University of Science and Technology**
Faculty of Agriculture, Department of Engineering, UST, Kumasi, Ghana

## Asia

**IRRI**
International Rice Research Institute, PO Box 933, Manila, Philippines.

**RIFT**
Research Institute for Fishery Technology, Jalan K.D. Tuban, PO Box 30, Palmerah, Jakarta, Indonesia.

**UPLB**
University of the Philippines in Los Baños, Laguna, Republic of the Philippines.
University of the Philippines in The Visayas Diliman, Quezon City, Republic of the Philippines.

# Europe

**FAO**
Food and Agriculture Organization of the United Nations, Fishery Industries Division, Via Delle Terme Di Caracalla, 00100 Rome, Italy.

**FPRD**
Food Production and Rural Development Division, Commonwealth Secretariat, Marlborough House, Pall Mall, London, UK.

**Humberside College of Higher Education**
School of Food Studies, Nuns Corner, Grimsby DN34 5BQ, UK.

**IDS**
Institute of Development Studies, University of Sussex, Brighton BN1 9RE, UK.

**ITDG**
Intermediate Technology Development Group, Myson House, Railway Terrace, Rugby CV21 3HT, UK

**NRI**
Natural Resources Institute (previously TDRI, Tropical Development Research Institute), Fish Section, Central Avenue, Chatham Maritime, Chatham ME4 4TB, UK.

# America

**IDRC**
International Development Research Centre, Box 8500, Ottawa, Canada.

# Australia

**University of New South Wales**
Department of Food Science and Technology, PO Box 1, Kensington NSW 2033, Australia.

For a comprehensive list of international fish technology institutes please refer to the FAO document cited in the list of further reading.

Printed in the USA
CPSIA information can be obtained
at www.ICGtesting.com
JSHW060043150824
68134JS00028B/2612